For the Love of Transformation

By: *Roger Love, Donna Maryanski, Jon Marino,*
Dr. Glenda Bradstock, Mannette Antill, Nancy Soulé,
Lindarae Polaha, Bettina Blanchard, Dominic Biscardi,
Christy Vermeer, Alicia Becerril, Kathleen Jones, Lisa Gray,
Lori Tsugawa, Dr. Marta Kassai, Maki Kajiwara,
Timothy Aleong, Dr. Caroline Stamu-O'Brien,
Adrienna Harris, Ken Patterson

Edited by: Elizabeth Garvey

Mastery of the Mind

Table of Contents

For the Love of Transformation

Introduction

Transformation is the fuel of life. While many people shy away from change, those who embrace transformation themselves, and those who chose to transform the lives of others, find the most fulfillment in life.

In the pages that follow, you'll find inspiring stories and practical wisdom from myself and my 19 co-authors who have experienced profound transformation in their own lives and helped guide others through change. From overcoming adversity and pursuing dreams to uncovering your authentic voice and true potential, these chapters offer a roadmap for navigating life's inevitable transitions with courage and grace.

While change can be uncomfortable, even frightening at times, it is also the gateway to new possibilities. The authors in this book demonstrate that by leaning into transformation rather than resisting it, we open ourselves to greater fulfillment, purpose, and joy. Their stories remind us that within each of us lies the power to reshape our lives, to evolve beyond perceived limitations, and to become the fullest expression of who we are meant to be.

My hope is that as you read these chapters, you'll be inspired to embrace your own transformative journey.

-Roger

For the Love of Transformation

The Sounds of Transformation

By Roger Love

Setting The Tone

As a voice coach, I've spent a lifetime helping people figure out what sounds should come out of their mouths. Sometimes they're singing, other times speaking. Over the years, some have labeled me a transformation expert, and I've never minded the sound of that phrase, or the implications it suggests.

Like any good coach, my success is all about helping people achieve their goals. I've often said that to change someone's voice, I need to change their physicality and mindset. So, I work on the voice, mind, and body, believing you weren't born with a voice; you were born with an instrument.

And unfortunately, there wasn't a manual in my crib to teach me (once I learned to read) how to tune and use that instrument to its fullest potential. I suspect you didn't get a manual either. Oh well, somehow, we survived without it.

But survival isn't good enough anymore with the way you use your voice today. I want you to LOVE your voice and use it to create the life you want. To accomplish that, you need to open yourself up to change.

Whether we realize it, moment by moment, each of us is changing. Some of us fight that idea, and others embrace it. Somewhere along our evolutionary journey, some have attached a negative connotation to the concept of change

5

and linked it with harsh realities, like growing old or losing someone you love. I propose we'd be much better off by embracing change and accepting it as a positive part of our human experience.

Let's label the specific change I've become known for as a vocal transformation. I listen to the way someone sounds and see if their voice is working for or against them.

When they speak, are they showcasing authentic emotions, connecting with people, and feeling confident about themselves and their message? When they sing, are they hitting all the notes without straining? Do they have a unique style, and are they moving people emotionally?

I spent 17 years only teaching singers. Then, famous speakers started asking me to work on their voices. At that point, I took everything I'd learned about singing and created a technique that would work for the speaking voice. I'd gotten quite good at helping singers make sounds that would influence millions of people, and I wanted to do the same thing for speakers.

And when I use the word speaker, I don't just mean famous people who get paid to use their voices. For me, anyone who opens their mouth and communicates is a speaker. On top of that, if anyone hears them, they are a public speaker, because the listener is the public.

So based on my definition, the world has billions of public speakers who need to find their voice, change it for the better, and use it to make personal and business life happen.

That's the transformation I'd like to help you with right now. Where do we start? By realizing that there are five key elements, you can develop and control your voice. I call them *The Building Blocks of Voice*. They are Melody, Volume, Pitch, Pace, and Tone. You'll need to learn each one if you want to be a better singer and/or speaker. Today, we'll focus on your speaking voice.

Melody

When you speak, even if you're not aware of it, you're attaching musical notes, pitches, to the words you say. Like a finger pressing down individual notes on a piano, your words move up and down the musical scale when you speak. That creates a melody.

Some melodies you use regularly are making you sound happy, sad, angry, or boring. To be an impressive speaker, you need to control how other people perceive you. I want them to see the best sides of you, and melody can help with that.

There are three types of melody:

Ascending: where you go from a low note to a high note as if you were walking up musical stairs.

Descending: where you go from a high note to a lower one, as if you were walking down the same musical stairs.

Monotone: Where you stay on the same note over and over as if you were a piano with only one key.

Most of us learned to speak melody by listening and imitating the surrounding people. We were also taught in school that when you had a sentence with a question mark at the end; you went up in pitch. When you had a period at the end of the sentence, you went lower in pitch.

The problem with attaching melody to grammar is that we've become restricted by our creative use of the melody. We need to be free to go up or down the pitch scale based on the emotions we feel and the words we choose to utter.

Along with that, listeners have attached certain melodies to specific emotions. When you use ascending melodies, people think that you're happy. When you use descending melodies, they think you're sad. And when your voice is monotone, it makes you sound boring.

So, here's what you need to focus on. I want you to add a lot more melody to your speaking voice. I want you to favor ascending melodies, use those the most. Stop overusing descending melodies. Stop making your voice go lower whenever you get to a comma or a period. There is no benefit to sounding sad, even if you're feeling sad. I'd rather you sound hopeful.

I'd also like you to eliminate being monotone. When you make the same note over and over, your listener thinks they know what you are going to sound like next, and then what you're going to say next. When that happens, they tune out and stop listening.

Start recording yourself speaking about anything. Then listen back and note how many times you used ascending melodies, descending ones, and how many times you stayed on the same note. You don't have to be a musician to hear those things.

The goal for melody is for you to speak with more ascending scales, less descending ones, and no monotone at all. Transform your awareness and use of melody. I know you can do it.

Volume

The next *Building Block of Voice* I want to focus on is volume. Too many people are afraid of being louder, thinking it makes them sound angry. But if you mix more melody in with the volume, you'll never sound angry, you'll just sound more confident.

Some years ago, a young woman came to me who wanted to be the first-ever female chair of the English department for the prestigious university she worked for. Her first problem was that the students didn't show her enough respect. They would come up to her after they received a graded test, and demand she raise their grade. She didn't understand why that was happening.

I listened to her speak, and I knew why. Her volume was soft, and she spoke airily. That combination of sounds is perceived as weakness. They felt they could overpower her to get a better grade. No matter how many times she said no, they kept asking.

I taught her how to speak with more volume and more edge. The edge countered the breathiness, and the volume made her seem stronger. Within weeks, the students stopped trying to manipulate her. Within months, she felt a new confidence in her voice and her life. Before six months passed, she became the first-ever chair of the English department.

Start recording yourself and experiment with more volume. Make sure you add in melody as well. Listen back and adjust. When you speak louder, it creates bone conduction, and it vibrates inside of your head, so it feels bigger.

Remember, your voice is not for you. It's for the people that listen to you. It may sound too loud for you, but perfect for anyone listening. That's what matters. Transform your volume, show people how strong and confident you are, and enjoy the benefits that come along with that.

Pitch

Do you have a low voice because you want to sound more masculine or older? Do you have a high voice that makes you sound younger than you are because you think it shows high energy?

Let's talk about pitch. In this example, it refers to the part of the range, low or high, that you hover around when you speak. Do you sound like Mickey Mouse or Minnie? Do you have trouble ordering pizza because your voice sounds like they need to ask for your parents' permission?

Most people think they're locked into whatever their voice sounds like from birth. When it's too high or low, they just blame mother nature and stay high or low. But that's an incredibly limiting belief and goes against my desire for you to transform your voice into one that you love, respect, and use to communicate your way into the conversations you want, the relationships you choose, and the outcomes you desire.

The main thing I want you to understand about pitch is that I want variety. I want you low, and high, and in the mid-range. I want the listeners to be surprised as you move up and down because of your changing emotions. Get higher when you're excited, and lower when you're more serious. I want to use pitch to show more of your authentic feelings.

A woman called me one day, and she sounded like an eight-year-old girl. When I asked how old she was, she said 37. That response would have made most people fall off their chair in disbelief, but not me. I've spent a lifetime listening to voices that are mismatched with the person speaking.

Her life was suffering because her voice was too high. She had trouble keeping relationships; she had difficulty with people taking her seriously at work, and she felt trapped, with no way out of the voice she was born with. I asked her if she wanted me to change it. She said, "Of course, I'm desperate."

I gave her a lesson, and within 30 minutes, she sounded her age, amazing, and was crying happy tears. She struggled in the days that followed the transformation, however, because the surrounding people weren't so open-minded. Her friends were so used to hearing her sound like a child, they were shocked and gave her negative feedback, such as "Who do you think you are?" and "Who are you pretending to be?"

That feedback was challenging for her to work through. She called me back and said, "I love my new voice, and you've ruined my life." I helped her make sense of it all, and the story ends happily. She adores her new voice and has used it to create a much better life.

I share this to help you understand that transformation sometimes surprises the people closest to you. But once they realize your change is for the better, the people who care about you will be supportive. In summation, regarding pitch, record yourself experimenting with all the range and feel free enough to explore all the possibilities.

Pace

Think of the last time you went to see your favorite singer or artist. Were you lucky enough to score Taylor Swift tickets? Did you secure seats for Bruno Mars? Maybe you went old school and caught the Def Leppard and Journey stadium tour.

No matter the performer, you'll notice that during their set, they mix it up. They play fast songs and slow ones, and some mid-tempo tunes as well. Why the variety? Because they don't want to bore the audience. I mention this musical reference to bring your attention to the pace of your speaking voice.

I know you're special, but most people end up speaking at the same speed most of the time without realizing it. Record yourself talking about something you love, and then something you love less. Play it back and note whether you kept your pace consistent or varied.

My suggestion is that you match the speed of your voice to your emotions. If you were a car, you'd be driving fast on the freeway and slower in school crossing zones. You'd be speaking faster when you got excited or angry, and slower when you were empathetic or sad. A brilliant speaker can showcase their authentic emotions, and changing the pace of your voice increases your chance of people knowing how you feel.

A client came to me with a problem. He was the CEO of a large company, having trouble communicating his emotions during large board meetings. His team said they only knew how he felt when he was angry. He had multiple emotions inside, but his co-workers believed he was mad all the time on the outside. So, I fixed his issue by adjusting his volume and pace.

He was natural, so I lowered that a bit, as high volume is certainly a component of hot anger. I also slowed him down. When you combine extra volume and fast pacing, you almost always sound angry.

I made those two remarkably simple adjustments, slower pace, and less volume, and he went back to his board meetings ready for action, connection, and emotion. A few weeks later, he called me saying he loved his new voice, and so did everyone at the office.

Tone

Have you ever heard the expression that more air means you care more? Well, I'd like to clarify that a bit. Some people believe that if they speak with more of an airy, whispery tone, it'll make others perceive them to be kind or empathetic. I don't agree with that.

Sometimes a bit of extra air sound, combined with other changes in melody, pitch, pace, and volume, can make you sound kind, sweet, but air alone won't do it. With that already said, let me tell you my definition of what I refer to as tone.

It's the amount of air or edge you hear in the voice. Say the word HAVE and hold out the A vowel, making it very breathy. That's what I mean by airy. Now say the word BRAT and hold out the sharp A sound and make it edgy and without air. That's what I mean by an edgy sound. I believe an influential voice has a balance of air and edge, and that's what I help people achieve.

A few years ago, a young emergency room doctor came to me. She was having voice and influence problems in the ER. It was often difficult for her to take command during an emergency. She felt like no one was listening to her. That situation was making it much harder for her to do her job and save lives.

I listened to her speak, and I realized the problem. Her tone was too airy. Let me explain a bit of the science behind sound projection. When you speak, the sounds and words are supposed to come riding out of your mouth on a solid stream of air.

When you have the right mixture of air and edge, that sound travels farther away from your mouth and vibrates the bodies of the people near you. If you speak with too much air and no edge, the sound comes out of your mouth and dissipates into the air before it reaches anyone else's body.

So, an airy voice does not physically connect you to others. The doctor's airy voice made her sound less confident, so the rest of the team didn't respond with action. I added more edge to her voice, which gave more volume. She sounded much more confident.

When she went back to the ER, her voice allowed her to lead her team and help more patients. I want you to learn from her experience. I don't want you to default to an airy voice because you're afraid to speak up. A great speaker exudes confidence, and I want that for you.

Till Next Time

In case you didn't already know, I want to save the world one voice at a time, starting today with yours. I want to make the word change synonymous with positivity and productivity.

Let's replace the word, whenever appropriate, with the word transformation. Because if you choose better, focus more, and control the transformation, you can become the best of yourself and help others.

Granted, there are certain aspects of being human we can't change yet. We can take anti-aging supplements, work out seven days a week, cut out sugar, reduce stress, but our end is inevitable. We will all expire one day in the future.

That's why I consider every day an opportunity for me to be better than the day before. Each day allows me the chance to transform, to experience more love, gratitude, and joy. Some days will be less than joyful, and I will embrace those as part of the journey as well.

Your voice is the perfect vehicle for transformation. It announces to the world who you are and what you want. Your voice can be the ultimate gift to the people you care about, and it can change the world for the better.

Now that you know all that, listen lovingly to the sounds you make, and create a new soundtrack for the movie of your life. You are music, song, emotion, and your voice matters.

UNMUTE YOURSELF and let the transformation happen.

About Roger Love

 Roger Love is recognized as one of the world's leading authorities on voice. No other vocal coach in history has been more commercially successful in both the speaking and singing fields.

When Roger was sixteen years old, he was already coaching groups like The Beach Boys and The Jacksons.

Over the years since, Roger has coached singers such as John Mayer and Selena Gomez, speakers like Anthony Robbins, sports stars like Tom Brady, and actors including Joaquin Phoenix, Reese Witherspoon, Zoe Saldana, Brad Pitt, Keira Knightly, Will Ferrell, Steve Carell, and Bradley Cooper. Roger coached Joaquin and Reese for the hit film *Walk the Line*, and she won the Academy Award for Best Actress.

Roger Coached Jeff Bridges and Colin Farell for the film *Crazy Heart*, and Jeff won the Academy Award for Best Actor. Roger's latest film credits are *Joker: Folie á Deux* (Warner Bros.) starring Academy Award winner Joaquin Phoenix, and Lady Gaga.

To get Roger's gift, go to: www.LOTbook.net/gift/Roger

For the Love of Transformation

Embracing Life's Transformations
By Donna Maryanski

There have been many transformations throughout my life. Some came out of learning lessons from not so pleasant experiences. Most came from my desire to grow and expand my mind, heart, and spirit.

I liken myself to the mythical phoenix who may crash and burn but always rises from the ashes as a new and better version of itself. The phoenix is symbolic of renewal, hope, progress, strength, and resilience.

As I approached retirement age and not being ready to retire, I challenged myself, prepared, and trained to do things I have always wanted to do, but fear and career had held me back. I took the no holds barred approach and set out to learn and prepare to address my lifetime lofty goals.

I am a trial lawyer and love what I do, so retirement because of age was not an option! Instead, I transformed my career as a defense lawyer to trying cases on behalf of the plaintiff.

Over the past two years, I focused on sharpening my trial skills and perfecting my presentations to juries, beginning with voice lessons from Roger Love. I dedicated myself to mastering the art of moving people emotionally with my voice, and it required learning many new techniques. Though I had spent my entire career speaking to judges and jurors effectively, these lessons allowed me to communicate at a significantly higher level, achieving a newfound effectiveness in my interactions.

I have put these new voice techniques to use in three trials so far. I achieved outstanding success for my clients in each of these trials.

As I embarked on this transformation of my speaking voice, I had many new experiences; working off a teleprompter, delivering a comedy routine, and singing a song I wrote. Now, I am afforded the opportunity to write a chapter in Roger Love's book.

I had always wanted to do standup comedy and sing in public, but I was bound by fear. Singing in public was terrifying. My knees were shaking so hard I thought the audience could hear them over my voice. After I did my standup comedy bit, I felt excitement and a surge of lightness.

My transformation experience has been enlightening and fun. I learned a better way to communicate with everyone. This brings joy to me and to those I encounter. What an enriching life lesson.

Changing the way I spoke had additional benefits. While well respected in my field, the number of speaking engagements tripled! I have a great sense of personal satisfaction knowing that I have helped educate the next generation of trial lawyers.

They say you can't teach an old dog new tricks—they were wrong! Transformation is possible at any age if you have an open mind and a willingness to learn.

Transformation is important to our general state of wellness. We need to be in search of personal betterment and new adventures. Transformation requires time and diligence to learning something new and internalizing it to make it become a part of you.

Through the investment of time, you learn whether a transformation is right for you. My advice is to persevere. Even if you decide not to go down that path, you have learned something new and are a richer person for that knowledge.

Not all transformations are life altering. You can have many mini transformations. Collectively, they allow you to grow new areas of personal and professional development.

Change is hard. My advice is to go slowly as the transition is much more natural and easier to incorporate into your personal life.

I believe that in every decade, you go through a transformation. Who you are at 20 isn't who you are at 30 or 40 and so on. You are transformed through your life experiences. How you accept and deal with these experiences is up to you. I can say that all my life's experiences have made me a great daughter, friend, lawyer, and wife.

I always knew I wanted to be a lawyer. It was my soul, so I had to find a law school that would let me work full time and go to school at night and on the weekends. I found my school. For over three years, I did nothing but work and study.

Becoming a licensed attorney was the greatest achievement of my life, and I felt like my journey was just beginning. When I entered the field, it was male-dominated, and women weren't often given the chance to try cases. But I was determined and eager to prove to them why I deserved to be in the courtroom.

With the help of my father, an already established trial lawyer, I read every trial book he advised me to read. I volunteered to attend various hearings during my time, all while maintaining my billable hours, to continue learning and gaining experience.

I took a note from John Gray's book *Men are From Mars, Women are from Venus*. In the book it says men want to be appreciated. So, I sought advice from all the male partners and let them know how much I appreciated their knowledge and willingness to mentor me. Soon I was attending hearings that more experienced lawyers usually handled.

At the end of my first year, I got my first solo trial. I had a goal, and I worked hard and learned as much as I could to get as much experience as possible. I won my first trial, and that set the trajectory for my career as a trial lawyer and pursuing my life's passion.

Now, I have tried well over one hundred cases. When people asked me when I was going to retire; I could only respond, "When I stop having fun." As of today, I am still learning and having the time of my life.

Despite being a successful lawyer, I fought a weight problem. I always felt that I didn't have the dates or the opportunities that people who didn't have a weight problem were afforded. It is my most painful lifetime memory. Sure, I tried every diet and was successful for a while. But I couldn't understand why sustained weight loss was not within my grasp.

Tony Robbins said that you won't make a change until you hit rock bottom. In my mind, I had been at rock bottom for many years. I had tried so many diets and exercise programs without success. I spent many nights crying myself to sleep over my failures.

One day, my mother had a health scare. They monitored everything she was eating and added one new food each day. In solidarity with her, I followed her doctor's plan. It was hard, but I was determined to be a good team partner for my mom.

Now it was time to find an exercise program. Enter the era of exercise videos! I could choose a program that was fun and fit my schedule. My mom and I started *Sweating to The Oldies* with Richard Simmons, enjoying our workouts with lively music. It was a game changer.

At the end of the video, various students who were much more overweight than I would come out showing a before and after picture of their progress. I cried tears of joy because I understood their struggle. Listening to the positive affirmations of Richard Simmons made me feel that I, too, was beautiful and worthy of a trim body.

I ate healthier than I did before and looked forward to my exercise videos. I didn't even realize I lost weight and inches. The process wasn't easy. I remember going to a store to buy clothes that fit. It was frustrating at first, as I did not know what size I was.

Then I remember going to my first court appearance. The old half-slip I had on under my skirt was too big. As I walked across the corridor to the courthouse, the slip fell around my ankles. I looked down in horror and then casually walked out of it and never looked back.

I finally had that thin body. This is everything I could ask for. Goodbye depression. Hello, new opportunities and even dates! Be careful what you ask for… This transformation, while a positive change, had some negative outcomes for which I was not prepared. Health-wise, I was fine.

But I never expected people to treat me differently. I was still the same person as when I had thirty more pounds on me, and it was disappointing to see the change. Before, no one was interested in dating me, but now that I'm thinner, suddenly I'm dateable. It made me feel like people didn't care about who I was—they were only interested in what I looked like.

People would often stare and look me up and down. I became very self-conscious about my body, even more self-conscious than when I weighed more. I started wearing clothing that was three sizes too big to hide my new figure. What I thought was going to be the happiest time of my life became one of the most depressing.

I didn't know what to do. I went through some counseling, as I didn't know how to deal with my new shape. Out of that, I grew and became more self-confident. I learned that my opinion of myself was the most important.

This transformation brought mixed emotions. I learned to embrace my new shape and identity, but it was difficult to accept that people who didn't like me when I was heavier suddenly wanted to date me, even though my personality hadn't changed one inch! While this was painful at first, it eventually became a blessing.

Continuing my career as a trial lawyer, I realized I needed a creative outlet. Always being a creative person, that side of me was still craving expression. I reflected on childhood memories, like when my mother would take me to the crystal and China department in the store. I'd be captivated by how the cut crystal sparkled, the light dancing off its facets. Even now, when I walk into those departments, I instinctively put my hands behind my back, just as I did back then, to fully take in the surrounding beauty.

I found a stained-glass shop near my home and fell in love with the colors and the reflective qualities. I began making art pieces for family and friends and eventually sold some of my work. Then, I entered competitions and am proud to say I am an award-winning glass artist. This creative transformation soothed my soul. Sometimes I would work on a glass piece and be so immersed in the project, I would look up and it would be well after midnight. There is a real peace and serenity in getting lost in something creative.

I never would have thought that I would teach various glass classes. I am living my best life ever! It would not have been possible if I had not allowed myself to be open to life's opportunities. While all experiences didn't start out as positives, there were life lessons that made me a better person.

My future transformation remains open. Life often brings unexpected opportunities, and being flexible allows us to embrace them fully. Beyond my love for glass art and my cocker spaniels, I have another passion: cooking. I'm skilled in the kitchen and am considering new directions, such as becoming a podcaster or creating cooking videos.

Sharing a meal is more than just eating—it's an act of love that builds connections and creates lasting memories. I'm excited about the potential of this next transformation and what it could bring.

Transformations can occur for a season, a reason, or a lifetime. Embrace these opportunities and learn from them. If they align with your needs, adopt them, even if only temporarily. Reflect on the knowledge gained from each transformation and use it to inspire those around you who are seeking their own changes.

I am deeply grateful to everyone who has guided, inspired, and supported me throughout my journey. Thank you for helping me become the best version of myself.

Transformations can occur for a season, a reason, or a lifetime. Embrace these opportunities and learn from them.

About Donna M. Maryanski

 Donna Maryanski has been a trial attorney since 1989, focusing on personal injury and employment law. She has tried over 100 cases, including 68 jury trials across California, dealing with matters such as auto accidents, wrongful death, and discrimination.

She holds a degree from California State University at Long Beach and attended Western State College of Law. Donna is an Advocate member of the American Board of Trial Advocates (ABOTA), serves on the Executive Committee for the Los Angeles ABOTA chapter, and co-chairs its Civility Matters initiative. She is also a faculty member for the 3-day Jack Daniels Trial Academy.

In recent years, Donna has presented on cross-examination, jury selection, and closing arguments at various legal events, including CAALA and Law Di Gras. She has chaired State Farm's CA/AZ trial academy for eight years and has spoken on handling expert witnesses and medical liens.

Besides her legal work, Donna volunteers as a pro bono mediator for the Los Angeles Superior Court. Outside of her profession, she is an award-winning glass artist, a gourmet chef, and a wine enthusiast, currently refining her pizza-making skills

To get Donna's gift, go to: www.LOTbook.net/gift/Donna

For the Love of Transformation

The Villains of Transformation

By Jon Marino

Trapped. Frustrated. Drowning in work for a client who doesn't give a damn. And where am I? In freakin' Hawaii, surrounded by paradise I can't enjoy. I'm sitting at a picnic table, lush jungle all around. I came here for inspiration, to reconnect with my creativity, and get some altitude on my life and business. Instead, I'm suffocating under its weight.

My team's stretched thin, standards sky-high, profits razor-thin. The beach I longed for might as well be on Mars. I'm caught in a brutal cycle of overwork and under appreciation.

For a moment, I consider throwing in the towel and surrendering to my villains by returning to the 9-to-5. Back then, I managed life support systems for babies and children under 18. The haunting alarms of those machines echo in my struggling business.

Then it hits me: I need a change, and it's not the job I worked so hard to escape from. And it's not just new clients—It's a whole new approach. You see, I was in the wrong business model, serving the wrong people.

I dig deep to identify my ideal client, uncovering their hidden struggles and secret desires. I craft an offer that truly helps them transform, wrapped in an irresistible message so compelling they'd crawl over broken glass to work with me. Test, validate, refine. The results? Overwhelming gratitude. Joy floods back into my work. Here's the kicker...

31

Had I quit, I would've missed striking oil by inches.

The lesson? Understanding your ideal client's deepest needs and crafting an irresistible message can transform your business. Small shifts in who you serve and how you communicate can yield dramatic results. Ready to transform your side hustle into full-time freedom? Let's dive in.

Picture this: You're burning the candle at both ends, juggling a side hustle while dreaming big.

Everyone could use your offer, right? Wrong. Casting a wide net leaves you drained, dealing with energy vampires who waste your time and resources.

Here's the secret: focus on your Aces. These dream clients need minimal effort, are a joy to work with, and yield the best results, fast. They're your golden ticket.

Think of it like a deck of cards—52 total, and only four Aces. All you've got to do is sift through 36 "bad" cards to find your winners.

Now...

I hear you barking, big dog; "52 minus 4 is not 36, no matter which school you went to." Of course, you'd be right. And yet when you aim for the Aces, you'll turn up the face cards along the way.

Sounds daunting? Stick with me.

All you need to do is start by answering three laser-focused questions about your ideal client:

1. Who Are Your Aces? Nail down their demographic. Are they business owners, parents, or singles? Knowing exactly who you're targeting allows you to speak their language and tell stories that hit home. (I'll share why that's important in a moment).

2. Who Are Their Villains? Identify both the struggles they openly discuss and the deeper issues lurking beneath the surface. This dual-layer understanding is crucial because it allows you to address their real pain points effectively. Keep reading, I'll clarify in a moment.

3. What Are Their Goals and Aspirations? Know what they're aiming for—whether it's financial stability or becoming a market leader. Their dreams and ambitions guide you in crafting offers that resonate deeply and keep them coming back for more.

Understanding these three key aspects of your ideal client can be transformative, and yet it's not always easy. Let me share a story that illustrates just how powerful this approach can be.

Roselito (Lito), an expert in Neuro-Linguistic Programming and hypnotherapy, openly struggled for four years to identify his Aces. What's worse is...

Deeper down, he felt lost and directionless. His business struggled to get off the ground despite investments in coaching and training.

My carefully crafted questions helped him identify his ideal clients. Together, we uncovered not just surface issues, but deep-seated needs and unacknowledged fears. Everything clicked. We also helped Lito define his brand identity and authentic voice for messaging that resonates with his ideal clients. Now, he attracts perfect clients with newfound clarity and purpose.

Your ideal client is the hero of their own story. Authors invest considerable effort in character development before writing. They often create extensive backstories and psychological profiles 100s of pages long. What if you sought to understand your ideal customer in the same way? By doing so, you can help your clients tell the best story possible.

About Those Villains

Every great story has a powerful villain. On your client's journey, these villains are their fears, frustrations, and pain points. Many business owners miss this crucial step, focusing only on benefits without truly getting their clients' struggles. They address surface-level problems, failing to connect deeply. Want to turn your side hustle into a full-time gig faster? Dive deeper. Understand the villains haunting your clients and become the indispensable guide on their hero's journey. The real power comes when you know there are three types of villains your ideal clients face. They'll tell you all about the first type, yet these are the least powerful villains. You might even consider these to be symptoms of the villains.

The second and third villain types are the ones that cause the challenges in your client's life.

Surface-Level Problems are the issues your clients openly discuss. They're immediate and easily recognizable, like struggling to attract clients or manage time effectively.

Deeper Issues are more ingrained and significant problems that often require introspection to uncover. Think of perfectionism or the endless cycle of preparation without action.

Subconscious Fears are the most deeply rooted and often hidden fears that drive behavior and emotional responses. Examples include fear of judgment or anxiety about being exposed as a fraud.

Stories and metaphors are powerful tools for addressing those deeper issues and subconscious fears that your clients might not even realize they have. Think of them as keys that unlock the hidden chambers of the mind. When you tell a compelling story or use a vivid metaphor, you're essentially creating a bridge between the conscious and subconscious. This allows your clients to explore their fears and challenges in a safe, relatable context. For instance...

A story about a caterpillar afraid to enter its cocoon can resonate with a client who's subconsciously terrified of change. By seeing their own struggle reflected in the caterpillar's journey, they can process their fear and envision their own transformation.

This indirect approach often bypasses the logical mind's defenses, allowing for profound insights and breakthroughs. Remember, just as a master locksmith handpicks the right tool for each lock, you must choose your stories and metaphors wisely to address the specific villains haunting your ideal clients.

Thinking back on Lito's journey—He was like a sculptor, standing before an uncut block of marble for four long years. The masterpiece within - his ideal client - remained trapped, obscured by layers of uncertainty and misdirection. He remained trapped because he was using the wrong tool. Each false start was a blow at the stone with a silicone spatula. Michelangelo, with a spatula, would just be another starving artist. Even Michelangelo needed a chisel.

When I handed him a chisel (guided by our careful questioning), he could cleave away the unnecessary stone with ease. The form within emerged - clear, defined, and full of potential. The transformation was more than uncovering his client's profile; it was about Lito rediscovering his own purpose and vision, transforming both his business and him in the process of creating the perfect...

Solution

Once you identify your Aces and their villains, the magic happens when you offer a solution that addresses their needs. Too many business owners cannot provide clear, actionable solutions, especially when starting out. This can leave your clients stuck, frustrated, and with unmet expectations. To jumpstart your full-time business, be the guide who helps them conquer their villains.

Here's how:

1. Identify and Understand Their Journey: Identify their "Now" and "Vision" with key milestones in between. Between these two points, identify the key milestones that mark significant progress along their transformational path.

2. Assess Their Current Position: Evaluate where the client stands on their journey at this moment. Identify their most pressing challenges and pain points, as these will be crucial in determining immediate steps. Also, take time to understand their current resources and limitations, as these factors will influence your potential solutions.

3. Provide an Immediate Solution: Offer a valuable, actionable solution to their most urgent problem. Show how it moves them towards their vision. Make sure this solution is valuable and can be implemented right away.

4. Guide Them to the Next Milestone: Connect your solution to their overall journey. Preview future steps and reinforce how each one brings them closer to their goal or away from their struggle, frustration, or pain.

You see... Once Lito understood his ideal audience's underlying issues and subconscious fears, he could craft content deeply resonated with them. He shared articles and videos addressing their villains, always ending with an invitation to a free discovery session.

In these sessions, Lito helped clients envision their future selves and pinpoint when in their past they conquered their villains. Armed with this understanding, he presented tailored plans for their transformation. He then offered his guidance on their transformational journey.

This approach, rooted in empathy and clear solutions, allowed Lito to naturally progress clients from free content to paid services.

By now, you've seen how crucial it is to find your Aces, identify their villains, and offer solutions that truly resonate. These steps are the foundation for turning your side hustle into a thriving full-time business.

The only question now is...

Are you ready to transform your side hustle into a full-time dream? Now, it's time to act and dive deep into your ideal client's world.

My team helps new businesses find the right words to turn clients into customers every day. Our Business Jumpstart answers a curated set of 50 laser-focused questions to help you unmask your ideal persona on a deeper level—far beyond just demographics. We're talking about diving into the secret motivations that drive their decisions to hire you.

It gives you an unfair advantage previously only available to our 7-figure business clients.

These are the same 50 questions we helped Lito answer, and it's your bridge from their "now" to the transformed life you can help them create.

With these insights, you'll craft messages so irresistible, your ideal clients will beg to work with you. Don't just dream about success—set this book down and visit **QueueSimple.com/Questions** right now to refine your messaging, target your ideal clients, and create solutions that address their deepest needs.

Why? Imagine waking up excited. Your side hustle has blossomed into a full-time dream, with a steady stream of ideal clients who value your unique expertise. Picture yourself turning in your resignation with confidence, knowing your business can more than replace your income.

You're no longer burning the candle at both ends, juggling your passion project with a demanding career. Instead, you're immersed in work that lights you up, your calendar filled with clients who are a perfect fit. Your family and friends marvel at your transformation. They see you fulfilled rather than stressed and overwhelmed.

Now, I'll tell you this...

After my realization in Hawaii, I knew I needed an adventure to myself. I heard about a Green Sand Beach at the south end of the island—one of only four in the world. Despite warnings about the difficult hike, I made the two-hour drive and set out on the three-mile hike. It was tough, yet when I rounded the last corner and saw that stunning emerald green sand–a hidden gem carefully tucked away between two massive cliffs.

I thought, "How many people missed out on this hidden gem because they're afraid of the journey?"

Just like the Green Sand Beach, your business is a hidden gem. Even the most stunning treasure remains undiscovered without a clear path. Your messaging is that path—guiding ideal clients straight to you, transforming a daunting journey into an irresistible adventure.

Every day you wait, someone misses out on your unique value. Are you ready to stop hiding and start shining? To turn your side hustle into a full-time dream?

The journey starts now.

Head to **QueueSimple.com/Questions** and craft the message that will illuminate your expertise. Your ideal clients are searching for what you offer. It's time to help them find you.

Your future self is counting on you. Let's make that future a reality today.

About Jon Marino

 Jon Marino is a man who has lived many lives. He's the founder of QueueSimple ("Q"-Simple)—helping 9-to-5ers jumpstart their entrepreneurial dreams.

Jon is a skilled copywriter, AI, and automation expert, digital marketer, published author, and leader of the Ignite Mastermind Phoenix chapter. Jon's expertise is both wide-ranging and deep.

He's a recovering civil engineer who re-careered to manage life support systems for babies and children on nightshift. There, he transformed his side-hustle into a healthy six-figure business. His journey from engineering to a successful entrepreneur exemplifies his versatile expertise and relentless drive.

At QueueSimple, Jon harnesses his extensive knowledge of AI, copywriting, marketing, business, and automation to empower aspiring entrepreneurs.

Did I mention... he plays a bad guitar, too.

To get Jon's gift, go to: www.LOTbook.net/gift/Jon

For the Love of Transformation

Chances and Choices

People and Events that Trigger Unexpected Transformation
By Dr. Glenda Bradstock

I had a lovely childhood, free of injury and illness. My parents were so incredibly supportive and encouraged me to be well rounded in music, dance, academics, and sports.

They came from farming families where they learned to grow their own food and eat well to stay well. They were self-sufficient and resilient. My parents lived by spiritual principles and healthy choices in food and lifestyle. I grew up with this influence—this "can do" attitude about anything I put my mind to.

Life was going great—I had graduated from college and ventured out into a career in photography and filmmaking. But when I returned to Texas to attend a friend's wedding, I was involved in a horrific car accident.

When I woke up in the hospital, I learned I had head and spinal injuries. I moved in with my mother to recover and ponder why this had happened and what I would do next. Carrying heavy camera equipment seemed impossible, not to mention the pain that it caused.

Then a few months later, a friend I hadn't talked to in ages called and asked me out for coffee. On the way to our destination, we made a stop at his Chiropractor's clinic.

The doctor treated Bob and asked, "Who's next?" I looked around and realized I was alone in the waiting room, and he

43

was speaking to me. So, I went into his office, and he briefly explained how he might help speed up my recovery. I agreed to come back for a complete workup and undergo treatment.

Within a few months, I had recovered and was doing photography again, but I realized there was something more for me now. I had been observing my doctor as he worked with patients and had time to ask questions.

He gave his patients back their lives, like he had done for me. I knew that if I had not discovered chiropractic when I did, my life would have been vastly different.

To capture beautiful imagery is one thing, but to help people get out of pain and regain their health really motivated me. I went back to school and after six years, I graduated and opened my practice. After I got my practice thriving, I took over my doctor's practice as well when he retired.

Fifteen years into practice, I sought some help from a pain management doctor. He was an anesthesiologist MD and did a special treatment with injections. I had had success with this therapy in the past. This new doctor took a more aggressive approach and accidentally burned the myelin covering of my nerves in my low back.

 As a result, my nervous system simply went to sleep from the waist down. The damaged nerves could no longer make the muscles work. The neurologist told me I would not walk again.

Despite the referral to a psychiatrist to help me accept my new fate, I simply could not believe this prognosis. I would not accept this as my future. I believed in my body's capacity to heal.

If given the needed nutrients and physical therapy, I believed the damage could be repaired. I put together a program that included nutritious food, exercise, meditation, and visualization.

I've always loved swimming in the ocean and walking along the beach. So, I would meditate and see myself walking on the beach, smelling the salty air, and feeling the warm sand beneath my feet. Then I would feel the cool water as I eased into the ocean waves.

I knew the body on a cellular level, so I would envision the cells repairing themselves, rebuilding the nerves and muscles to make it possible for me to walk again.

Slowly, over the months, I progressed from a wheelchair to a walker with leg braces, then to a cane. And I walked on the beach again. That was my vision. And I could go back to what I love—taking care of my patients.

Years later, a boyfriend from 25 years before sought me out for help, as he had had a major health event that had put him in a wheelchair. After working with him to walk again, we fell in love and got married.

We travel many months during the year, so I retired from the physical practices and continue consulting and teaching wherever we are. While we travel, I work with patients on Zoom to regain their health.

After taking a complete history, I order comprehensive testing to make a proper diagnosis and set up a plan for their recovery. These patients might not have realized, like some of you reading this now, how remarkable the body is at healing, if given the right support.

Detailed food plans, nutritional support with supplements and an individualized exercise plan lay the groundwork for recovery. Your body has an amazing capacity to heal, if given the chance.

So, I would like to share with you some basics. I teach my patients to get well and stay well.

Nutrition

A well-balanced plan of unprocessed foods is vital to recovering and maintaining health. In my programs, protein is essential for building and repairing tissues. They also help in making enzymes and hormones supporting the immune system. Protein in some form is essential for everyone.

As you age, getting adequate amounts of protein is critical for growing and maintaining muscles, so you can stay active and independent. I recommend animal proteins in the way of lean meats, fish, eggs, and dairy as the major sources, while legumes, tofu, nuts, and seeds are supplemental sources.

Fruits and vegetables are a rich source of vitamins, minerals, antioxidants, and fiber. They are a substantial source of carbohydrates for energy. Getting a daily variety of colors in vegetables assures that the immune, reproductive, digestive systems, the heart, and brain are supported.

Mixing an assortment of the colors of red, orange, yellow, green, and purple in your meals ensures you are getting all the vitamins and minerals. Vegetables are alkaline, which helps to balance the body from other acid-forming foods.

Healthy fats provide energy, promote cell growth, and make absorption of fat-soluble nutrients possible. Avocado, nuts, seeds, fatty fishlike salmon, tuna, mackerel, and sardines provide healthy fats. Using olive oil, avocado oil, and coconut oil in recipes and in cooking is an easy way to get healthy fats.

Each component of the food plan contributes to the overall functioning and health of the body, so incorporating a balanced mix of proteins, fruits, vegetables, and healthy fats is essential for optimal health.

Hydration

Drinking filtered water throughout the day supports the digestive system by helping to dissolve nutrients and allow them to be absorbed more effectively. Cognitive function also relies on adequate hydration for concentration and memory. Dehydration can make you feel tired, so that might be a cue to drink more water.

Blood volume and blood pressure depend on adequate hydration throughout the day. Toxins are normally produced by all the chemical reactions in the body and those can be eliminated in fluids not only by the kidneys and the bowels, but by respiration and perspiration.

Remember, water makes up about 60% of your body on average. The amount of water you need may vary based on age, weight, climate, and physical activity levels. Half your body's weight in ounces is a good starting point.

This amount should be adjusted for the increased amount of physical activity and hotter temperatures. Eating fruits and vegetables with high water content, such as cucumber, watermelon, and oranges, also contributes to your daily hydration needs.

Exercise

Moving your body is so important to physical health, mental well-being, and overall quality of life. Exercise enhances cardiovascular health. It strengthens the heart and improves blood circulation. It builds and maintains muscle mass and strength.

Weight-bearing exercises like walking, running and resistance training strengthen bones and reduce the risk fractures from osteoporosis. Yoga and stretching enhance flexibility and balance, improving mobility and reducing the risk of falls.

Respiratory function is enhanced by power walking and aerobic exercise as it improves lung capacity and efficiency. More oxygen circulating in the blood boosts the immune system, making the body more effective at fighting off illness and infection.

Warm up before you exercise and cool down afterwards. Try different exercise at least two times during the week to start.

Listen to your body. Sitting long periods at a desk takes its toll. Stretching, pulling your shoulders back and taking a few deep breaths go a long way to maintaining focus and productivity.

Quick burst of intense activity, like running in place or jumping jacks for 30 seconds to a minute, works too. No equipment needed.

Working at a computer or scrolling on a phone, you lean the head forward, which puts a strain on the neck and upper back. When you are in a seated position, blood flow is restricted to and from the legs. Sitting long time increases the load on the spinal disks, especially in the low back.

A standing desk or a sit-stand workstation allow you to alternate sitting and standing to remove some of that pressure.

There are also mental benefits from exercise. Physical activity increases the production of endorphins, the body's natural mood lifters, which helps reduce stress and anxiety levels.

Exercise can ease symptoms of depression and improve your overall mood and emotional well-being. Increased circulation supports brain health, improves memory, attention, and decision makings skills. It may reduce some risk of cognitive decline.

Sleep

Sleep plays a crucial role in maintaining overall physical health and cognitive function. During sleep, growth hormones are released to promote tissue growth and muscle repair. Hormones that regulate hunger are released while you sleep to control appetite and weight maintenance.

Consolidation of memories occurs while you are sleeping, transferring them from short-term to long-term storage. This is essential for learning and keeping information. When you are sleeping, the brain clears out the waste-products, including beta-amyloid, a protein linked to cognitive decline. Being alert and in control allows you to be independent.

Nature

Being in Nature can have many benefits for your health, both mentally and physically. Being exposed to UV light for 20 minutes without glasses activates the immune system. Spending time outside in the daylight can lower levels of cortisol, the body's stress hormone. Exposure to natural environments can lift the mood and reduce feelings of anxiety and fatigue.

Natural settings can induce a state of relaxation and calmness, which promotes healing. Walking outside is a good way to get the multiple benefits of nature, fresh air, UV light and exercise.

Breathing

Inhaling brings in the oxygen necessary to support life while exhaling releases the unwanted byproducts of the chemical processes going on inside the body. Stop for a moment and notice how you are breathing. Is it shallow from your chest or deep from your abdomen? Periodic conscious breathing is healthy, both physically and mentally.

I recommend from yoga deep belly breathing using your diaphragm to expand and contract on each breath cycle—out when you inhale and in when you exhale for several cycles.

Alternate nostril breathing from yoga also changes the blood pH and harmonizes the right and left hemispheres of the brain, energizing the body and the mind.

Meditation

Meditation promotes a sense of calm. It activates the body's relaxation response, reducing the production of cortisol, the stress hormone. Mindfulness and being present in the moment come with meditation and enhance your ability to concentrate and be more productive.

Increased resilience allows you to cope with challenging situations and adapt accordingly. In a relaxed state, your circulation increases, your muscles soften, and your digestion improves, leading to better healing.

Visualization

Having a vivid picture of your desired physical goal can significantly increase the likelihood of achieving it. Make your vision as detailed as possible, adding color, sounds, emotions, physical sensations, smells, and tastes. Energize your vision, see yourself in the picture, and visit it frequently.

I encourage you to try some of these ideas in your life to get and stay healthy. There may be physical challenges in your life. Remember, when you have your health, you have a greater capacity to navigate those challenges and become vibrantly healthy and resilient again.

About Dr. Glenda Bradstock

Dr. Glenda Bradstock, DC, is a highly experienced Doctor of Chiropractic and Functional Nutritionist, bringing 42 years of expertise to her practice. She earned her BA in Philosophy from Mills College and the Doctorate of Chiropractic and Functional Nutrition from Texas Chiropractic College.

Dr. Bradstock Specializes in helping individuals who are experiencing burnout and exhaustion because of chronic health issues. Through comprehensive testing and personalized care plans, she identifies and addresses the root causes of her patients' conditions, enabling them to regain their vibrant health and energy.

Besides her clinical practice, Dr. Bradstock is a coauthor of the best-selling book, Thinking on Purpose: A 15 Day Plan to a Smarter Life. She is also a certified Dream Builder Coach and Life Mastery Consultant from The Brave Thinking Institute.

With a passion for holistic health and wellness, Dr. Bradstock is a trusted resource dedicated to empowering her patients to thrive in all aspects of their lives.

To get Glenda's gift, go to: www.LOTbook.net/gift/Glenda

For the Love of Transformation

Empower Your Voice to Unleash Your Vision

By Mannette Antill, Founder, Your Voice Connection

"Mannette! Lower your voice!"

I was only about four years old. I remember the penetrating glare in her eyes more clearly than my mother's words. They say the eyes are the windows to the soul, but with her cold icy glare, the windows to her soul shut behind an impenetrable iron door.

Instantly frozen, my breath stopped. My mother was my world, and her acceptance and approval were my center and my safe space. I had to get her back - so I risked it all and desperately tried...humor!

"Is this low enough, Mother?" I asked, teasingly taking my voice as deep as a four-year-old can, down deep into my throat, but in what I suddenly realized was a dangerously saucy tone. And again, my breath stopped. But then, with excruciating slowness, there came a sliver of light and warmth in her eyes and finally the burst of a chuckle as she answered, "Yes!"

In a great wash of relief, my breath erupted in a giggle. And, for a while, it became a bit of a game. But at four years old - that's where my voice stayed—deep in my throat.

And those parental corrections disappeared as I learned to keep my voice buried in an armored little body as my entire being became smaller and smaller and my power diminished. The demand to lower my voice was clearly a directive to bury the power of not just the sound of my voice—but my authentic inner voice and its free expression.

You see, a small and buried sound comes from a tightly bound inner voice. Your unique identity and power become buried in a tightly bound body as you learn to sculpt your sound, your body, and your very being to gain the approval and acceptance you desperately need to survive as a child.

And that acceptance seeking behavior becomes habitual, even as you grow in stature and experience. You continue to be shaped by this embodied need for approval to feel safe.

It was not an unpleasant voice. Low in pitch, breathy so as not to be demanding, and certainly not confrontational—just the voice a sweet little girl from Texas needed to fit into a world that wanted her that way. And my mother proved to be a powerful example.

Don't get me wrong, Southern women, even in the 50s, were powerful, and my mother held her own. But you had to be "genteel" and avoid appearing "confrontational," always offering the men a way to grant your requests while preserving their sense of strength and control—and doing so in an "acceptable" tone.

My mother was certainly well-intentioned. She deeply believed she was preparing me for "success" in a world she knew and understood so well - a world where even other women were put off by "pushy" women. So, I learned to walk this talk and talk this walk.

I was not a withering violet. I was confident (ergo my need to be quieted and controlled.) But I learned to be "successful" by adopting and achieving goals that would allow me to get the approval and acceptance I craved and needed as my armor.

That same year, when my father graduated with the college degree he attained on his World War II GI grant, we moved hundreds of miles away from an extended family that had shaped my world. Then we moved again, and again, and again as my father fought the demons of his traumatic war experience. No one knew about PTSD in the 50s and 60s. But his children did. And I grew in my ability to adapt.

Lauded for being so adaptable and sociable. I learned quickly just who I had to be to fit into each new school, and I learned exactly how to move into the "right" group and please and get the approval of classmates, teachers...and my parents.

I learned well how to play a part. Chosen for debate and theatrical competitions, I sang in a varsity choir that went on a European tour. I was a dancer, played the flute and was an award-winning baton twirler. I held classroom and school offices throughout high school and college—even during the 50s and 60s when girls didn't do those things as often.

But I did it all sweetly and politely and with such decorum because I was such a "good girl." And whether these "achievements" arose from my own deep desires, they were the things I could do that brought me the approval and acceptance I craved. I was a virtuoso adapter!

Then in the 60s I became caught up in the massive social tumult of civil rights and anti-war protests of my era. Our feminist consciousness awakened, and we coasted with the Second Wave of feminism as we realized that "sisterhood is powerful."

I pivoted and became a political science major. And after graduation, worked as the administrative aide to a Texas legislative committee on which sat Sarah Weddington, the young 26-year-old lawyer who had won the landmark "Roe v. Wade" abortion rights case at the U.S. Supreme Court.

I abandoned theater, music, dance, and the arts and I went to law school, where I believed I could make the greatest impact to bring a change in the world. And, not coincidentally, it was also where I could continue to find the acceptance and approval I still so deeply craved. I would do and be something important!

My law class had only 16% women, but we founded the Women Law Students' Association and sued the five largest law firms in Dallas for sex discrimination. After law school, I helped found the Women in the Law section of the Texas Bar and served as its second president.

I worked as a civil fraud prosecutor with the Texas Attorney General's office and then as a corporate in-house attorney for a Fortune 500 and a Fortune 50 corporation. I held leadership positions in the Texas Bar, the Dallas Bar, and in the community, served as the legal advisor to a domestic violence shelter, and co-founded organizations focused on advancing women's legal, educational, and political empowerment.

Then, after practicing law for six years, I had my first child and another two years later. I delivered my children at home with a midwife, a decision met with disapproval, as did my next decision to move to the beat of my heart.

I left my hard-won corporate position to establish my law firm with another woman who also had children. We enjoyed sharing that our mutual midwife helped "birth" our practice, incorporating and advising women-owned businesses.

But despite continued success, I struggled with the adversarial nature of law, which demanded constant battle and confrontation. The inner voice that craved authentic expression in dance, music, and acting refused to remain silent.

I finally left the practice of law to become the Executive Director and Media Spokesperson of the local American Civil Liberties Union. This allowed me to focus on using my voice rather than legal skills, but confrontational advocacy was still required.

I had a third child, and yes, I went home. Later I would have a fourth, with the help of my former law partner, turned certified nurse midwife. Then, at age 45, I had my fifth child.

I had feared proving the perception of male power brokers that women "couldn't cut it," that they would "give up" and go back home. I fought feeling I "owed it" to other women to stay the course.

But I finally realized that the freedom and power I so fiercely sought for women had to be grounded in the freedom to choose. Freedom and power did not have to rest in adopting the choices others might approve of and even admire.

Moving to Connecticut and then Los Angeles, I used my new freedom and my diverse experience to advocate for my children, and others, when two of mine were assessed as neurodiverse. I helped found a non-profit school and programs for special needs children. I also joined a puppet troupe to sensitize children to the dignity of the differently abled.

At 58, I returned to school and began my extensive study of theater, discovering a newly empowered voice that I devoted to moving hearts and minds through the arts. I learned that foundational voice work reveals all.

Misogyny and discrimination were rampant in the years I practiced law, and over and over I would offer contributions in boardrooms that were, within minutes, repeated word-for-word by a man and met with greater approbation. But when

I pivoted from using my voice at the Bar to on the stage, I realized that my deeply lowered voice might very well have played a role in how I was perceived and heard.

I once strove to create change with legal power. Now, with over a decade of experience as an actor, theater producer, and teaching artist, I bring a unique blend of artistic insight, professional training, and personal experience to my new passion: empowering purpose-driven entrepreneurs to become transformational speakers.

I help them bring the change for which the world awaits and that only they can deliver with their unique talents and gifts and with powerful, resonant, authentic, creative, and inspiring voices.

My training lies in the voice and speech methodologies taught in the most well-respected acting conservatories across the globe and created to empower and feed creative free expression. And now, I bring an empowered voice no longer tightly armored and without the need to gain the approval of others to achieve acceptance.

I also trained in the powerful voice work of Roger Love. And I am one of his certified practitioners offering his extraordinarily accessible gateway methodologies to a full and resonant voice, where singing and speech combine as we share his mission of "transforming the world one voice at a time."

Which brings me to YOU!

Because only if YOU embrace your own one-of-a-kind sound and your own empowered voice and passion with your unique gifts, visions, dreams, and goals will you reach the full potential of your power.

Training the actor's voice involves a deeply somatic and embodied experience, merging mind and body as one. Unlike the cognitive and the intellectual learning experienced to develop your professional skills; these body and vocal energies reduce the cognitive load on your brain.

This allows you to engage with text in a playful, curious manner, free from judgment, keeping your expression fresh and alive, and aids in memorization.

You remember your content while expressing it authentically and powerfully in-the-moment. Staying open to your intention, breath, body, and feelings creates a genuine connection with your audience.

You expand your range in pitch, pace, tone, volume, and melody organically, and this authenticity is what they hear, remember, and value most.

As you learn to trust yourself and your new skills, you can move beyond fear, allowing a spontaneous swirl of in-the-moment expressions. This creates a constantly evolving dance of physical feelings, breath, movement, and emotions, resulting in unique, powerful creative expressions that are always fresh, exciting, and vital.

Imagine stepping onto a stage, open, relaxed, and ready to perform. Stand tall, knees free, body free, and feel the energy coursing through your body like a gentle current. Open yourself to your in-the-moment experience.

Visualize yourself buoyantly swaying to invisible energies and melodies, as joyful and free as a bubble, graceful as a feather. Feel the radiant vibrant energy of excitement and anticipation.

Embody the potent power of a commander or the intensity of an emotion that brings you to tears. These are embodied expressions—tapping into your authentic self and infusing your breath and words with vitality.

Actors say, "Your body is your instrument." Breath creates vibrations in your vocal cords. They resonate through your head, down your spine, deep into your body, and out -where they touch your listeners, sending ripples of energy, empowerment, and creativity through your audience.

As you navigate the intricacies of embodied communication, you embark on a journey toward self-discovery and transformation. And through practice, patience, and a willingness to play, you unlock the true essence of human connection.

In the end, it's through the embodiment of your authentic self that you breathe life into your words, transforming the world, one vibrant communication at a time.

If my experience of having my voice suppressed and disempowered led me to seek pathways of discovery and empowered me to share these opportunities with others like you, what other life could I want? Certainly not one rooted in seeking acceptance and approval from others.

My journey has shown me the profound impact of embracing and trusting one's authentic voice. It has allowed me to connect deeply with my true self and inspire others, like you, to do the same.

Follow your own empowered voice and transform the world!

About Mannette Antill

 A voice, speech, and presence coach, award-winning actor, theater producer, teaching artist, and lawyer, Mannette has used her communication skills in courtrooms, Fortune 50 boardrooms, and as a media spokesperson on camera, television, and radio.

She now empowers purpose-driven entrepreneurs to become transformational speakers, rediscovering their unique voices to communicate with confidence, authenticity, and creativity. Her Be the Voice of Change programs, rooted in methodologies taught at the most esteemed acting conservatories, empowers clients to move past the fear of public speaking and deliver impactful presentations.

Her education includes Classical Acting at the Royal Conservatoire of Scotland and Master Class and repertory work at Will Geer Theatricum Botanicum and more. She is a certified teacher in Fitzmaurice Voicework and Vocal Yoga and is a Lessac Kinesensic Facilitator. Her life, as diverse as her career, has included twirling fire batons and barrel-racing horses. Married since 1981, she cherishes her five children, two stepchildren, and twelve grandchildren.

To get Mannette's gift: www.LOTbook.net/gift/Mannette

For the Love of Transformation

Finding Your Groove: Life's Improvisation

By Nancy Soulé

Transitions are hard. Imagine yourself snuggled up in your cozy bed, toasty beneath the covers on a bleak morning. That blasted alarm pierces the quiet, insisting that it's time to get up, get going, rejoin the human rat-race. That secure cocoon providing a safe harbor for your dreams and imagination is sadly, only temporary.

An awakening to reality forces you to pry open your eyes and take some action. It is an absolute necessity. You are given only one life, and it must be embraced while you can. Staying in bed is not really an option for very long—you have to pee, get that irresistible cup of coffee, or feed the dog. Another day begins, providing opportunities for daily adventures, whether planned or spontaneous. Don't fight it, embrace the opportunity! You never know what adventure lies ahead.

Transformation is a bigger challenge. It too is completely unavoidable. You can't stand still. Like a seed bursts into flower, the sun rises, and hordes of people launch fourth into that new day, you too are afforded the opportunity, nay the privilege, to take advantage of yet another unique chance to become whatever you may have defined as your ultimate potential. You have a choice every day to determine your own direction, and create that potentially surprising, unique, and new beginning.

In the day's design, you fulfill an image of who you think that you have become. Some people face surprising challenges in health, family, or occupation, and they bravely overcome tremendous adversity with determination and courage. Others are comfortable tackling smaller goals and remain content with those achievements. But either situation offers opportunities for tremendous personal transformation.

We all began somewhere, and even after eons of human existence, the source is still up for discussion. But it is completely impossible not to transform. You must grow from infancy to puberty, from childhood to adulthood. You have the same number of minutes in a day, days in a month, and months in a year, for as long as you live. Whether you believe that destiny is predetermined, or that you have the freedom to choose, transformation is inevitable. But you can decide how it will develop based on your mental attitudes and how you choose to manage them. Is it a mess? Or is life sending you a message?

I grew up with a passion for music and it has always been an inherent part of my being. By driving my family crazy with my incessant singing, I, like any child, insisted on repeating certain songs over and over again, ad nauseam. I remember riding in the car, bursting into song and being told that no one could sing along with that; start it in a different key. What? There was more than one? And I discovered I could even make up my own songs! I did not know the rules yet; apparently that is something you learn in your progress, regardless of the field.

I had a piano teacher who encouraged creativity, but when I wrote chord a transition she didn't like, I was told, "Oh no, you can't do that! Use this chord to follow that one." What? Why the heck not? I liked the way mine sounded, but it didn't follow "the rules." How often in life has this scenario kicked you in the head to say, "Stop that! It's not 'the right way!'" But to your mind, it's YOUR way, so why can't it be right?

Those childhood transitions, the "rules," subconsciously affect your personal transformations. Those channels of restriction determined your ultimate voice. But the universal truth as I see it, is that you inherently just want to be heard, you want to be seen, you want to be celebrated for your ideas and your voice. I have traveled the world and seen for a fact that regardless of country, nationality, race, religion, or current economic situation, everyone has the same desires: to be safe, to be loved, to be acknowledged, and appreciated. Finding your own voice is essential to contributing your own uniqueness to the world. You have important things to say!

As an ambitious musician, I took the path to progress through imitation, mimicking my teachers and my idols. As learners, we search for that ultimate comfort zone of confidence that assures us we are "doing it right." But there comes a time when discovering the genuine joy of the process is in finding your own voice, and overcoming that fear of judgment from others, by truly being who you are and claiming your own singular glory. You must create your own melody. Go ahead, use that chord! Sometimes, "Rules be damned!"

I was taught, I learned, I copied. I danced with my hairbrush "microphone" and sang to the radio, mentally "becoming" others in my head. But with each new phase of life, the growth path continued past the popular musical idols of my teens and college years. The idols changed, but I still sought "the voice."

I found that ultimate artistry comes with the dedication to discovering how to break the rules to transform. Beethoven, as a child prodigy, conformed to the demands of his teachers. But when he changed the rules, he became a legend. What he did to classical music was akin to the expressive process of contemporary jazz. He improvised. His physical deafness locked him within his world of musical magic, and he was driven to write it down before it drove him completely crazy. He gave birth to fresh sounds that were revolutionary for their time. He couldn't be afraid of the reactions of others. For one thing, he couldn't hear their opinions, nor did he care. He channeled what he heard, and it had to be as it was. He had his own voice, and that was all there was to it! Through that commitment to his own uniqueness, he transformed musical history for all time.

Life itself is "jazz." Every day you are offered the opportunity to play the notes of the songs you are given as written, to do the job as prescribed. You feel the need to follow the rules of whichever game you are playing in life to conform. But often, you are forced to improvise. Life has a way of throwing you curve balls, leaving you stranded on base, or sometimes even striking you out. How you react and change the game to suit the challenges creates the melody of your days and scores the music of your life.

In the book, *The Power of Music*, Elena Mannes says, "Scientists have found that music stimulates more parts of the brain than any other human function." Music fires up both sides of your brain, revives memories, and gives you confidence. Music is active sound therapy for a plethora of mental, physical, and emotional conditions; an essential and powerful healing practice.

Playing with others amplifies that power. According to Keith Richards of the Rolling Stones, "There's a certain moment when you realize that you've just left the planet for a bit and that nobody can touch you. And when it works, baby, you've got wings. You are flying without a license."

As a performer, you become an instrument of the music and have the freedom to break the chains of dictated rhythm and words to express the deeper feeling underneath. It's not about you as the player, but about becoming a channel of emotion, allowing a liberation from self to serve the moment and the message through your own unique and distinctive expression.

As in life, so in music, it is imperative to LISTEN to others and respond to their input and accompaniment to create a conversation. Getting out of your head and into the music is the path to releasing yourself from the comfort zone of predictability to explore the world of other ideas, other cultures, and broader points of view. The ultimate joy is getting past the *"me"* to revel in the power of the *"we."*

My personal passion for music led me along paths with massive opportunities for improvisation in life. I got married, as it seemed to be expected. I played the notes as written, but I was singing someone else's song, dancing to their tunes, and fitting into a pre-written score.

In search of my voice, I joined an a cappella group, a blues band, and then a corporate party band, and all provided opportunities for expanded repertoire. But in it all, as a short, white girl, I was expected to imitate Michael Jackson, Aretha Franklin, and even James Brown... I hadn't found "me" yet!

But then, I found jazz. I was there that at last I was granted permission to discover my voice. In jazz, the performer has an opportunity, nay the obligation, to "break the rules" to create something unique. The rules of rhythm and melody no longer constrain the performer and allow the ultimate flexibility and creativity to create a variety of emotional impact.

If finding musical freedom is your intension, I would suggest that if you have performance aspirations, there are a few ways that you can find this liberation in life. To take wing as a musician, I can recommend three basic paths that you might follow to let your voice be heard, be it instrumentally or vocally. Each path has its unique challenges and advantages. If music is in your soul, let it out. The world needs to hear it!

The path to freedom is in practice. Grasp the opportunity for transformation to grow from a scared wannabe performer to the cool, confident professional that is living inside you.

Here are some ways to get your voice heard and get paid for it. To accomplish any aspect will require the process of mental transformation to break out of your comfort zone. So, throw off the covers, get out of bed. Let's go!

One: Local hometown gigs. There are many websites and Facebook groups for access to others who want to play for fun and potential profit. Choose the music that suits your personality, musical tastes, range, and skills. If you are an aspiring, ambitious singer, test out your skills with some karaoke to break the ice and help determine what fulfills your soul and what genre rocks your world. It's ok to start with imitation where it suits you. It is all part of the path to finding yourself. It's what you do with it later that will shape you.

Find players that complement each other. Search out small venues that offer live music for your style where you can entertain. This will require time for practice, proper preparation and rehearsal, and some research.

With a local band, you have the chance to play with others, expand your repertoire, sharpen your skills, and broaden your horizons. And a bit of extra income (don't play for free) will provide some encouragement and personal validation for you to support your progress.

Two: Join an established band that may be touring. If your skill set is adequate to tackle a bigger endeavor, online sites provide access to opportunities. Life has a way of moving us in and out of things, and players rotate, allowing vacancies that need to be filled. Find the one that suits your musical style and aptitude. Don't be afraid of auditions! That's the best way to see if the situation is the best fit for you and for the others in the group. The perfect band is looking for you.

These groups will have a predetermined set list and a performance format. But an erratic schedule of locations may challenge the rest of your life plans. The repertoire is predictable, which makes it easy to be proficient with repetition, but it can become redundant. If travel is involved, it will require repeated packing and unpacking, adapting to various locations, and a constant need to be flexible and adaptable to change. But that is part of the adventure.

The benefits are the consistent opportunity to play and travel. A manager will handle the paperwork and money, and the pay is often better than the local pub may offer. Be responsible, available, proficient, reliable, and consistent in performance. Good chops are essential and adaptability to people and circumstances is also crucial. Others count on you to be there and be ready. Keep the drinking to a minimum. Enjoy the ride.

"Being apprehensive about a new experience is natural and even expected, but exhilaration often follows."
- Dean Gualco, Making a Difference

Embracing the ultimate transformation from wannabe to professional takes a leap of faith in yourself, and knowing that you have built the skills to be who you imagine yourself to be. To take yet another step to musical freedom, here is another option that might appeal to you, or someone you know with an adventurous spirit.

Three: Play your music on a cruise ship. There are over 1000 musicians hired every year to fulfill the roles open on over 350+ cruise ships sailing the world's oceans. There are many opportunities for performance as vocalists, bands, and instrumentalists with the right skills.

This scenario requires commitment as you may be away from home for extended periods, from two weeks to nine months or more. This floating city will require life aboard a huge floating metal box with personal space limited to tiny accommodations, often shared with others of various nationalities; like music college life on steroids in some ways.

But the benefits will provide an amazing opportunity to progress from that role of local hometown performer to the level of consistently paid professional, while being granted the opportunity to see the entire world. You play every day, receive a consistent paycheck for that time onboard with no overhead for room, food, or health care. You travel the breadth of the world, and ports range from Shanghai to Santorini, Anchorage to Auckland, or Venice to Vanuatu.

You play and live with many nationalities, share expertise, perspectives, and cultures. You are no longer a weekend warrior, but have become a proficient, confident, exceptional, and worldly professional. And the bonus is the opportunity to explore the ports of the world.

Granted, this is not a life that suits everyone and favors only the truly adventurous, fit, and flexible. However, if you want to break the mold of a predictable life, you'll find details in the books *"Work at Sea, See the World"* and, specifically for musicians, *"Notes That Float."*

If you prefer a personal guide through the process, explore the *Global Musician Program: Notes That Float* for an in-depth look at life onboard and the ultimate in musical expression, coupled with the benefits of global travel. For more information, visit www.NancySoule.net or email me at MusicianSupport@NotesThatFloat.net.

The world needs your talent. Celebrate the path at every turn and express the power of your unique voice. You are exceptionally valuable and must be heard!

> *"You have a treasure within you that is infinitely greater*
> *than anything else the world can offer."*
> -Eckhart Tolle

Whatever your choice of expression, let your transformation be a vehicle to transform the world with the power of your unique and distinctive voice! Get up. Get out. Go do it!

About Nancy Soulé

 Nancy Soulé is a distinguished author, speaker, and vocalist with over 30 years of experience in the music industry. Her multifaceted performance career has ranged from a cappella to big band jazz.

Her innovative course, *The Global Musician Program: Notes That Float*, empowers adventurous professional musicians to maximize their talents on a global scale, providing opportunities for exclusive positions on cruise ships.

Nancy has authored several influential books, including *Work at Sea, See the World: An Insider's Guide to the Working Life on a Cruise Ship*, and *Notes That Float: The Ultimate Musician's Guide to Getting Paid on Cruise Ships*, are invaluable resources for musicians navigating the complexities of the cruise industry.

With her extensive knowledge and experience, Nancy Soulé inspires and guides musicians to embrace worldwide travel, fostering a community of passionate artists that sets her apart in both entertainment and travel as she facilitates intercultural communication and international empathy.

To get Nancy's gift, go to: www.LOTbook.net/gift/Nancy

For the Love of Transformation

Own Your Voice and Live R.E.A.L.

Rooted—Expressed—Authentic—Life
By Lindarae Polaha

Losing My Voice

As they wheeled my gurney down the corridor to the operating room on that fall day in 1996, I did not know that the same surgeon who would be operating on Julie Andrews several months later would also bring my singing career to a screeching halt. I had high hopes that after the flat fluid-filled polyps on both of my vocal cords were removed, my voice would be stronger than ever, allowing me to leap into the full operatic career I had trained for and was anticipating.

But sadly, that picture of hope never came to fruition. Following a long healing process, I was left with poor functioning vocal cords on the inside and a raspy frog-like sound and very limited range on the outside, telling the tale of a poor outcome.

Prior to surgery, I was so careful not to tell anyone of my vocal health issues for fear of blackballing myself in the music industry. That silence turned out to be very costly.

Just a few days before my procedure, I met world-renowned voice teacher William Riley, not understanding at the time that he could have helped me heal without surgery and who later, thankfully, was integral to regaining my voice. If I had known world-renowned vocal coach Roger Love at the time, he too could have provided me with a vocal lifeline.

As my voice was not improving, I tried to leave no stone unturned in my desperate attempt to find a doctor who could help. I spent countless hours with the most respected voice specialists in the country. In the end, I stopped singing, rested, and let my voice continue to heal. It was one of the toughest decisions of my life to walk away from my dreams; all the time, effort, energy, money, and advanced degrees to move forward in another direction. Yet, here is where the true journey to finding my voice began.

Reclaiming My Voice

Fast forward several years. As I sought to learn more about my post-surgical vocal cords from leading laryngologists, I finally came face to face with the truth. My vocal issues and ultimate injury stemmed from inefficient breathing.

At first, this made no sense at all. Singing is all about the breath. Without breath, there is no sound. But as I realized the amount of tension I held in my body, trying to capture the essence of the sympathetic "freeze" response, I saw how I was fighting against myself.

The self-preserving instinct inside me said to be still and stop breathing, fearing the proverbial tiger about to pounce and consume me if I made a sound. It was as if I wasn't even there.

Unknowingly, I worked very hard to overcompensate. As I look back in time for signs, I remember instances before training to be an opera singer when I had difficulty blowing up a balloon — the air just wouldn't come out. Or times when

I tried to scream on a roller coaster, and nothing came out. I'm amazed that I could sing as well as I did for as long as I did before the vocal problems began. There comes a point when compensatory efforts break down and fall apart. Unaddressed unconscious forces bubble to the surface.

Shortly after my mother passed away, I was facing the reality that I had built a life for myself that was based on what I thought other people wanted for me. I realized just how silent I had become, so much so that I found myself in a dark place with few options.

It was during this time that I met master coach and bestselling author Nancy Levin and began healing my heart through coaching. Layers of wounds buried deep in my subconscious were asking for attention and love that only I could give.

As I dove in, Nancy shared the concept of underlying commitments, a concept she learned from her mentor and teacher, bestselling author, and transformational coach, Debbie Ford. I discovered I was more committed to silence than to making the loudest sound possible without electronic help through operatic singing. The commitment I made to myself as a child to stay safe through silence and invisibility was winning out.

Little did I know the havoc that was boiling up inside demanding to be heard. It wasn't until I truly embraced all of who I am that I could let go of my stronghold on silence, own my voice and re-inhabit my life.

This process of digging deep within to root myself in the truth of who I am, leaning into expressing that truth vulnerably and inhabiting the full essence of my being authentically allowed me to step powerfully into the center stage of my life and really live! In this way, I could truly own my voice and live R.E.A.L., a Rooted Expressed Authentic Life.

Rooted—Tune in and Listen to Your Gut

Being grounded and rooted in your own truth will provide the foundation to remain true to yourself, regardless of circumstances.

For most of my life, I was not connected to myself, trying to be what I thought others wanted me to be, to feel loved and accepted. As I experienced various traumatic events in my life, I continued to fracture away from and abandon myself. When I finally dug deep within, I discovered the greatest source of love and acceptance had been inside me all along.

Like a tree that sources life-giving nutrients from the soil, I discovered that I too could know my own needs, what is ok and not ok for me, and source my sense of identity from inside.

When I am tuned into this internal compass, I can feel what is a full-body yes and what is a full-body no. When I don't heed the warning signs, like in my story above, I later pay the consequences. But when I listen and act, my life feels so on track. I feel strong, like a deeply rooted tree that will not fall over when stormy weather and turbulent winds come up.

What are the nutrients that I source from deep inside? They are some of my most basic needs, like acceptance, love, and approval.

Knowing that I can give myself the love and care that I need is like tuning into an internal navigation system that shows me the next step forward, shifting from autopilot to the driver's seat. The freedom that comes from self-sourcing what I need, as opposed to looking for validation and approval externally, is freedom on a whole new level.

And the best part is the consistency. When I look to others for approval, the fear of losing love and acceptance is always present. But when I'm self-sourced, if there are lapses, I can address them myself by examining my life, seeing where there is a kink in the line, a doubt, a fear, a self-judgment or shame, and reconnecting to my truth.

With this deep-rooted self-assurance, it is possible to inhabit life from a grounded sense of being in the world and withstand whatever life brings.

Expressed—Speak Your Truth

Connection to your inner voice, the truth of who you are, opens a channel for true communication.

Having a voice is more than just emitting a sound. It is self-connection that validates your very existence.

The physical voice is created by the vibration of the vocal cords in your throat as air (breath) moves through the cords. The inner voice is the innate cellular information created as you were formed in the womb — all the natural human instincts that strive to nurture, protect, and guide you.

As young children, we look to caregivers and our environment for validation and a sense of worth and often receive conflicting information. As we try to make sense of the world so we can feel safe, loved, and accepted, we learn to override our natural instincts. Our new tendency becomes to hide and stay quiet.

Remember the tiger lurking that is waiting to pounce and devour? To express, we need to breathe. Breathe into our being, into our gut and heart, into the essence of who we are.

As we inhale, inspiration flowing through us begins the cycle towards expression. Yet there are different ways of breathing; a high, shallow fight or flight sympathetic way and a low, deep, more relaxed parasympathetic way. When breathing in a calm, full-body breath down to the belly, there is more than air connecting to our body. Inspiration, breathing in and connecting to the spirit within, and exhaling from our very life force.

When exhaling from this place of spirit, engaging intuition, heart, soul, and gut, there is a vulnerable presence that can be felt by those within hearing and feeling distance. This is an expression that connects.

I believe people want to feel and connect at a deep level, even though it may seem scary. When someone speaks or sings, it can either be a set of sounds or a vehicle for feelings and connections between heart and soul.

It's important to acknowledge feelings being communicated, both by the other person and us. This acknowledgment is knocking on the heart door and asking for a connection.

True communication is when one heart connects with another heart. This is truly being heard. When we own our voice at this level, genuine connection becomes possible.

Authentic—Stay Present

Presence is key to being able to feel heard, be heard, and hear others. When we are rooted in who we are and able to express that, we can then be authentically present.

If we are not present in our own life, it's difficult to hear others. When we listen from a void, where we need to be heard ourselves, we may only hear what we want to hear or what fits into our belief about others not hearing us.

When we are not present, the words are being said, but there is no connection, nowhere for the words to land. If we want to listen from a place of not needing something from the person we are trying to listen to, we must first tune into our own heart and gut and hear ourselves. When we no longer have a need for others to hear us, we can listen objectively with empathy and compassion, and there is a place in us for what the other person is saying to land.

Authenticity begins with self. Be in the presence of yourself and get to know yourself. No one else can truly see, hear, or know you if you do not first see, hear, and know yourself.

Authentic is what happens when you can, even if for a moment, let go of fear, judgment, and shame and lean into the genuine essence of who you are. When you know who you are, what you want, and can stand in that truth, then the channel is open.

From this sourced, genuine place, you can make choices that support you. The first step is to tune into your inner voice — your heart and gut — and allow yourself to see and hear your own truth. It may not feel comfortable to show your truth to others and the world, but being able to be present and see it in yourself first is where it starts.

Life—Stand Your Ground

Once you are rooted in who you are and able to express that authentically, you can then stand your ground and live life on your own terms as the person you truly are.

When you source life from within — your gut, heart, mind, and all your senses — what does that look like?

Your gut intuition is the fertile soil of natural instincts and a sense of identity. Your heart has both feeling and intelligence and is the crossroads at the center of your being that provides both guidance and direction. The mind has perceptive qualities and can decipher and discern based on feedback from all the senses.

If your life has had its share of difficulties, I firmly believe that the more pain, hardship, and challenge you have experienced, the more potential there is for joy, happiness, and expansion. Not that you want to invite more negative experiences in, but that they come with the gift of greater empathy and compassion, not only for you, but for others and the world.

Standing in the essence of who you are, you can then lean into the full-body yes cues or take heed of warning signs that inspire doubt and concern. This is living life from a consciously tuned-in place.

Losing my voice represented being disconnected from myself, from my voice.

As I mentioned at the beginning, I didn't want to be blackballed, labeled as damaged or different from the status quo. Afraid to be anything less than perfect.

Yet, what if my life experiences and all the qualities that make me who I am are my superpower?

If I can allow myself to be vulnerable, seen and heard, then I can connect with others who may relate to those experiences and qualities.

Connection to others begins with a connection to self.

Abandoning yourself may have felt necessary for survival and safety. Yet as you re-inhabit your life, hearing your own truth is the first step to real safety — being rooted in the truth of who you are.

To be fully present in your life, it is necessary to root into your feelings and authentically express them in a vulnerable way. This will allow for deep connection to yourself and others and provide a place for your voice to land, take root, and connect.

Owning your voice and living R.E.A.L., a Rooted Expressed Authentic Life, is what's possible when you fully inhabit your life and live in the true essence of who you are.

About Lindarae Polaha

 Lindarae is a coach with over seven years of experience in guiding individuals to navigate between where they are and where they want to be so they can break free from limitations, discover what is possible, and powerfully step into the life they desire.

Lindarae is a Certified Life Coach through the Ford Institute and Levin Life Coach Academy, a Certified Roger Love Method Coach for Speakers, and holds an MM in Vocal Performance from the University of Nevada, Reno, and a Professional Studies Certificate in Vocal Performance from the Manhattan School of Music.

Through her coaching, Lindarae empowers clients to connect to the voice of their heart so they can fully express all of who they are and feel truly heard. She specializes in providing tools and insights necessary to get unstuck and unlock true potential. Her compassionate approach fosters a safe environment where clients can explore their deepest desires and aspirations, ultimately leading to profound transformations.

www.LindaraePolaha.com

To get Lindarae's gift: www.LOTbook.net/gift/Lindarae

For the Love of Transformation

Tap into a Tidy Life

By Bettina Blanchard

I'm a sucker for transformation. From the chaos of *"before"* to the ahhh of *"after,"* it makes me feel good. It must be the big hit of dopamine I get whenever it's time for the *big reveal.*

When I learned that my voice coach and mentor Roger Love was co-authoring a book on transformation, I was all in. I've made a career out of helping people tidy up and I want to share what I've learned about transforming a home from chaotic and stressful to peaceful and easy.

Your home can be so much more than a roof over your head. I believe it plays an important role in enjoying life to the fullest. Especially when you *love where you live.*

That's when your home welcomes you inside; when you have in it what you need and love, it's easy to find your things, and then put them away. When it's satisfying to maintain your home, life is better. Life is easier. Life is more fun.

Let's start by naming the elephant in the room. I'm referring, of course, to **clutter**.

Clutter in your home doesn't happen because you don't have enough storage, haven't found the right container or installed a proper closet system. Those are challenges of the head and clutter is one of the heart.

Clutter results from our love affair with stuff. We love to shop for it, purchase it, collect it, make it, give it. However, you

91

may struggle to find a workable strategy to let go when something no longer serves you. And unless you get rid of things at the rate at which you accumulate them, you will have clutter in your home.

What is *clutter* exactly? It's the things you **don't** use or love **but can't let go.**

Maybe you have clutter hiding in your drawers, closets, garages, or it's right out in plain sight. Either way, it's likely causing you some amount of discomfort, even pain.

Clutter is expensive. You not only paid for it, but you also pay to keep it. I don't just mean in offsite storage units, I am talking about rent, mortgage, insurance, oh my.

Clutter wastes your time. You spend hours searching for something you know you have somewhere.

Clutter makes even simple tasks more difficult. From cleaning and laundry to cooking and dishes. If there's too many coffee cups on the shelf, who wants to empty the dishwasher?

Clutter can make you feel overwhelmed, distracted, isolated. When you're surrounded by cluttered surfaces, there's no room to work. It's hard to stay focused. You don't want to invite people over. Who wants to feel that way in their home?

Clutter is **not** simply mind over matter. Your things **can** become attached to your heart. Trying to convince you to "just let go of something" doesn't work. I know, I've tried.

The truth is we all have things in our homes we're not using, we don't love, but we just can't bring ourselves to say… **"I don't need to keep that."**

Instead, we say,

> *"You can never have too many of those."*
>
> *"This will be useful someday."*
>
> *"I paid a lot of money for that."*
>
> *"It was a gift."*
>
> *"It's an heirloom."*
>
> *"They don't make it like this anymore."*

Sound familiar? I still say these things because sometimes they are true.

Emotional attachment to objects makes it difficult to let go. And so, you don't. It's easier to hold on to *everything* than it is to decide about the hard stuff. Before you know it, you feel totally overwhelmed in your own home.

Perhaps you're afraid of forgetting a special person or a memory? Maybe you don't want to hurt someone's feelings? Or you feel an obligation to keep heirlooms to honor your family.

Whatever your reason for keeping things you don't use or love, it's the negative emotions (often fear) that cause your body to generate cortisol. It's known as the fight, flight, or freeze response.

Cortisol and fear have kept us alive. When you are in a negative emotional state, the primal part of your brain is running the show. But most of the time, keeping clutter isn't a life-or-death decision.

So how do you move forward? What you need is a simple home organizing system to follow and tool to help ease the emotional ties when you're stuck.

Enter SOS and EFT-A Heartfelt Pairing

SOS is my simple 3 step system to organize your home. Sort. Organize. Simplify.

The Emotional Freedom Technique (EFT) also known as tapping, is a mind-body tool used to help people relieve overwhelm, anxiety, depression, and stress.

How do they work together? Having a simple system to follow takes the guesswork out of organizing your home. It's your track to run on.

Tapping is a tool to help you act when you're stuck. Maybe you're so overwhelmed you can't even start? When all you can see in your home is the emotional sticky stuff, tapping can come to the rescue.

Let's first look at the SOS three step system.

Find any pile of clutter and then follow these simple steps:

Step 1. Sort: Remove things that are no longer relevant or don't belong in this space by answering the following 3 questions:

- **What stays?** You love it, use it or both.
- **What goes?** You don't love it. You don't use it. It's broken, obsolete, or redundant.
- **What lives elsewhere?** Useful, relevant items that belong to someone else or live somewhere else and are just not here.

Step 2 Organize: Now that you have created space, put your system in place for the things you want to keep following three rules:

1. Keep like items together.
2. Give everything a home.
3. Use labels.

And answering four questions:

1. **Who** uses the space? Take them into account.
2. **What** is being stored? Choose your containers and systems accordingly.
3. **Where** is the best place for this to live? Maybe it's always lived here, but things change. Is there a better place somewhere else?
4. **How** frequently is it being used? Give the easiest accessible real estate to things you use daily.

Following these rules and answering these questions will help you customize your home organizing system for success! Now you're ready for step three.

Step 3. Simplify: This step is part habit and part mindset. It's how you stay on track and maintain your new system.

The Habits:

Habit #1. Don't put it down, put it away. When you have a system and you know where it belongs, it's easy to do.

Habit #2. Sweep your space. Look for things that were left out or put down and re-home them.

Habit #3. Edit constantly. We are forever bringing new things in. Make sure there is room for the new. Exercise your editing muscles and eliminate the excess.

Habit #4. Make the things you need to do easy to do. Clarify the process and simplify the steps.

The Mindset:

Your mindset around stuff can change. Be open to keeping less and notice how life in your home becomes easier.

Say yes to less. Everything you keep owns a little part of your brain. Don't be afraid to say no or no thank you.

Want more time? Keep less stuff. The more things you keep, the more time you spend either organizing, maintaining, managing, or searching, stressing, or buying.

Now you have a simple home organizing system, but what do you do if you feel so overwhelmed you can't even start? Or you're holding something you don't use or love but can't let go?

EFT to the Rescue

Emotional attachment to stuff happens to most everyone and when it does, you need a tool that will bring clarity to your decision making and help calm your nervous system. That tool is called the Emotional Freedom Technique or tapping.

Maybe thoughts like *"what if I need this someday"* or it was a gift or handcrafted heirloom? It may not "spark joy" but it evokes emotion, feelings, and memories, happy or sad, that cannot be denied.

Your brain doesn't work its best when you're in a negative state. Stress, anxiety, overwhelm, grief, can all cause your body to produce cortisol, making you want to fight, flight or freeze.

Tapping on acupressure points while experiencing negative feelings sends a calming signal to your brain, which dials back cortisol production and allows you to have a more thoughtful response.

The creative, resourceful part of your brain now considers different solutions and outcomes besides just the need to hold tight and hang on.

Tapping is the action you **can** take when you get stopped by the words in your head. Tapping gets you out of your head and back into your body. The result helps you find your solution to your problem. It's not someone else telling you what to do.

How Do You Start?

Where in your body do you feel stuck? How strong is it on a scale of 0-10 (being not stuck at all, 10 you feel you can't move?)

Whatever thoughts you have that are holding you back, say them out loud while you tap lightly 10-12 times on each point.

You can use these words as a guide to get you started tapping. Your own words have the most power.

Eyebrow: I'm so overwhelmed.

Side of Eye: Where did all this stuff come from?

Under Eye: There is so much stuff in this house.

Under Nose: Where did it all even come from?

Under Lip: It's too much work.

Collar Bone: I don't have enough time.

Under Arm: Even if I had a whole day, I'd never finish.

Heart Point: There's just too much here.

Top of Head: I am so overwhelmed.

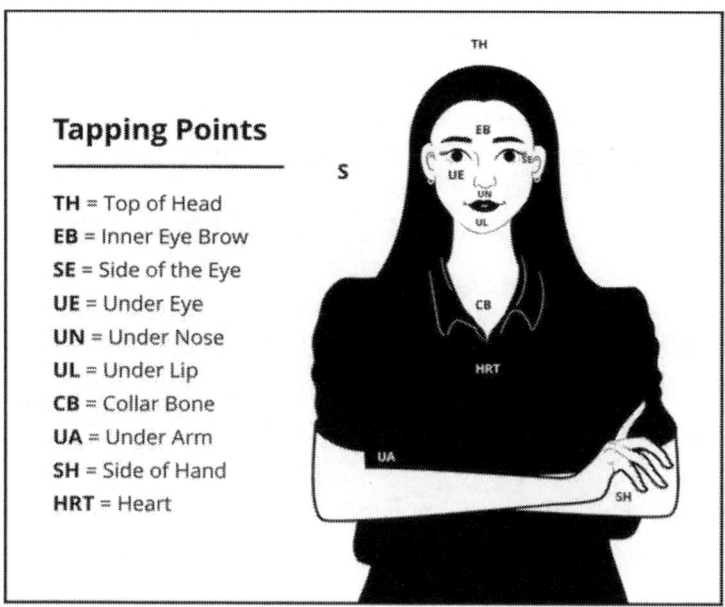

Tapping Points

TH = Top of Head
EB = Inner Eye Brow
SE = Side of the Eye
UE = Under Eye
UN = Under Nose
UL = Under Lip
CB = Collar Bone
UA = Under Arm
SH = Side of Hand
HRT = Heart

Tapping through the ten points takes only a few minutes. Do this at least 2-3 times. What's your number now? Don't stop too soon. You can repeat the same words or change them. What matters is they ring true for you.

Then take a deep breath and ask yourself if you're ready for the "maybe" round which might sound like this...

Eyebrow: *I am overwhelmed, but maybe I could start small.*

Side of Eye: *Maybe I could set a time for 10 minutes and start.*

Under Eye: *Maybe I could just pick the low-hanging fruit.*

Under Nose: *Maybe I could take the dishes to the sink.*

Under Lip: Maybe I could pick up the trash & recycling.

Collar Bone: Maybe I can pick up the things that got put down and put them away.

Under Arm: This didn't happen overnight. Maybe I can plan to turn this around.

Heart Point: I'm not the only one who struggles like this.

Top of Head: Maybe I can cut myself some slack and take a step forward.

Tapping on **Maybe** makes it possible for you to take small steps. And the small steps add up. It's how anything large was ever accomplished. One small step at a time.

Now you have a simple system to follow and a tool that can help get you out of your head and back into your body when you get stuck.

Celebrate your success no matter how small. Forgive yourself right now for your clutter. You're a good human. I know you are. And you're on the path of becoming the best version of yourself you can be. Go you!

About Bettina Blanchard

 Bettina Blanchard is a Home Organizer, Teacher, and EFT Tapping Coach with over 20 years of experience in the field. She is the founder of Bettina & Company, where she passionately helps individuals struggling to maintain a tidy home by teaching them effective strategies and mind/body techniques to release clutter with ease.

Bettina holds a master's degree in Organization and Management from Antioch University Graduate School, equipping her with the skills and knowledge to address the complexities of home organization from both a practical and psychological perspective. Her innovative approach integrates traditional organizing methods with Emotional Freedom Techniques (EFT) to create a holistic system that fosters lasting change.

As the creator of the *Tidy Tapper Method*, Bettina empowers her clients to not only declutter their physical spaces but also to navigate the emotional barriers that often accompany disorganization. Her unique blend of expertise allows her to guide individuals through a process that promotes mindfulness and emotional well-being, transforming their homes and enhancing their quality of life.

To get Bettina's gift, go to: www.LOTbook.net/gift/Bettina

Flourish Beyond Limits

By Dominic Biscardi

Have you heard the popular adage that success is not a destination but a journey? Most agree. Why? This journey is transformative—an adventure, a quest paved with many moments that shape a character and offer continual preparation for each new pinnacle.

Success is not a stagnant stop on the roadmap of life; it is a free-flowing highway running its course without containment. If you allow it to do so, the journey will transform struggle into soaring, mediocrity into extraordinary, and languishing into flourishing. This transformation is not just a possibility; it's a certainty.

The secret is to keep going and push past self-limitations. There is no area out of its ascendancy—family, friendships, career, education, self-development, and faith. However, as you may already know, it is not automatic, and you cannot stay stuck.

The pursuit of excellence, the desire to thrive, and the aspiration for achievement demands fortitude, a deliberate strategy, and relentless effort. Success cannot be attained without it.

Some say that success leaves clues, so there are proven keys that unlock the steps necessary to elevate your life to the next level. Break through the barriers! With the right applications, you can go from someone who ekes out an existence to an individual who excels with vibrancy and purpose.

Three Keys to Your Journey

1. The Power of Vision

"Vision is the art of seeing what is invisible to others."— Jonathan Swift.

Emphasizing the pivotal role of vision in the journey to success serves as your North Star, illuminating the path towards dreams and ambitions. A clear and compelling vision not only provides direction and purpose but also helps align your actions and decisions with your long-term goals. It fuels motivation and resilience, enabling you to overcome obstacles and setbacks with determination and optimism.

Vision shapes your mindset, and the converse is just as true. It fosters a sense of meaning and fulfillment as you are driven by a deeper purpose that transcends the mundane. By articulating and committing to a powerful vision, individuals and organizations inspire collective effort and collaboration, harnessing the potential of a shared dream.

It not only charts the course but also empowers you to envision possibilities beyond your current reality, propelling you towards extraordinary achievements and a brighter future. You must see it before you can see it. If you can see it, you can achieve it.

Strategies:

- Set Specific Goals: Have a target.
- Create a Vision Board: Keep it up and in front of you.
- Speak it Forth: Use affirmations and attach emotion.
- See it: Visualize the outcome as you desire it.

2. Advance through Adversity

"Adversity builds muscle. Adversity creates strength. Adversity is a preparation for success."—Andy Andrews.

Advancing through adversity means progressing in life despite facing significant opposition, challenges, or obstacles. It involves not only enduring tough times but also growing stronger and more capable. You must keep hope alive and focus on favorable expectations.

Hope plays a crucial role by extolling the belief that better times are ahead, that your future is secure, and that your purpose remains intact. Adversity is a part of any significant achievement and comes to challenge a great calling. You must stand resolute and allow hope to set tomorrow's forecast.

A daily cadence of well-thought-out actions is essential to prevent stagnation in these times. Establish a routine of consistent, purposeful, planning to help ensure progress. Whether it is dedicating time each day to your work, self-care, learning, praying, meditating, or networking, these small, regular efforts accumulate over time—compounding and leading to substantial advancement.

Adversity tests your resolve—your metal—and it builds resilience, causing the powerful attribute of fortitude to rise to the surface of your heart. Advancing through adversity means acknowledging that setbacks or roadblocks are temporary and can be overcome with perseverance, determination, and, most importantly, love. They do not have to detour, detract, or keep you down—you have everything within you to get back up and resume your race, moving forward toward the gold.

Strategies:

- Keep Hope Alive: It is your anchor.
- Develop a Growth Mindset: Learn, develop, and work it.
- Learn from Failures: They are inevitable, but neither fatal nor final.
- Stay Persistent: It often separates successful from unsuccessful.

3. Prepare and Maintain a Positive Attitude

"Attitude is a little thing that makes a big difference."— Winston Churchill.

Preparing and maintaining a positive attitude impacts transformation, stress reduction, and creating a flourishing environment. It cultivates adaptability, enabling you to pivot when necessary to embrace change and challenges with optimism and enthusiasm. Pessimism and despair take a back seat.

A positive attitude is not merely mind over matter, but a conscious, concerted effort based on a confident outcome despite what may peer at you now. Properly placed, it exudes an atmosphere where creativity and collaboration blossom into a realization that today is temporary, and tomorrow is on the horizon. The best is yet to come.

Maintaining such an attitude not only facilitates the path to personal and professional renewal but also inspires and motivates others. It contributes to a supportive and dynamic experience. It is the seedbed for true transformation. Some added benefits are unlocking joy, promoting happiness, uncapping motivation, and enhancing overall mental well-being.

Optimism has been linked to better health, both mental and physical. It allows one to live and experience life with greater confidence and enthusiasm.

Strategies:

- Practice Gratitude: Shift your focus to what is right.
- Surround Yourself with Positivity: Engage with people who inspire.
- Focus on Solutions: Free your mind to receive the download.
- Study Success Stories: Read Widely, Reflect Often, Rewire Intentionally, Repeat Hourly.

If we take a brief look into the concept of flourishing from the Latin word "floreo" which means to bloom, presents a state of vitality, health, growth, and success. It is not merely existing but thriving to reach a sense of wholeness. According to Dr. Martin Seligman, a leading figure in positive psychology, flourishing goes beyond happiness, defining flourishing through his PERMA model—Positive Emotion, Engagement, Relationships, Meaning, and Accomplishment.

Seligman states, "Well-being cannot exist just in your own head. Well-being is a mix of feeling good and having meaning, good relationships, and accomplishment." Corey L. Keyes adds that flourishing is "a state where people experience positive emotions, positive psychological functioning, and positive social functioning, most of the time."

Achieving your full potential requires pushing past mediocrity and striving for excellence. Flourishing is not just about surviving but thriving in every aspect of your life. It's about living with purpose, passion, and perseverance.

To flourish means to thrive or develop healthily, particularly when nurtured by a supportive environment. In positive psychology, flourishing denotes optimal human functioning. So, achieving excellence requires a balanced approach to life.

Take care of your physical, mental, and emotional well-being. There are practical steps. Physical activity enhances your energy levels, mood, and overall health. Mindfulness techniques such as meditation and deep breathing reduce anxiety and increase mental clarity. Last, prioritize rest to ensure you get adequate sleep and take breaks to avoid burnout.

Denis Waitley said, "View life as a continuous learning experience." Flourishing, along with excellence, commits to continuous learning and self-improvement. The world around you is evolving and expanding. Keeping your edge requires a proactive approach to gaining new knowledge and skills.

John Wooden said, "It's what you learn after you know it, all that counts." In this age of information, where everything is a click, tap, or voice text away, excuses are eradicated. Learning has never been easier—it awaits your eager curiosity.

Stay true to your values throughout life's journey. Identify what is most important to you and align your actions with those values. Engage in team and community activities that provide comfort and guidance, such as sports, outreach, or church services.

Serve others—give back to your surroundings or abroad. Acts of service enrich your life and provide a sense of fulfillment.

Relevant Inspirational Quotes and Stories

Ronald Reagan: "The greatest leader is not necessarily the one who does the greatest things. He is the one that gets the people to do the greatest things." Reagan's leadership style was contagious and empowering, encouraging others to rise to their potential.

John F. Kennedy: "Ask not what your country can do for you— ask what you can do for your country." Kennedy's call to action inspires us to take responsibility and contribute to the greater good.

Kim Perell: "You have to believe in yourself when no one else does—that makes you a winner right there." Perell's journey from being laid off to becoming a successful entrepreneur highlights the power of self-belief.

Roger Love: "You have a voice. It matters. Your voice can inspire change." Love, a renowned voice coach, emphasizes the importance of expressing oneself confidently and authentically.

Jaime Kern Lima: "Don't just aim to be successful; aim to be significant. Aim to make a positive impact on the lives of others." Lima's success with IT Cosmetics underscores the importance of purpose-driven work.

Johann Wolfgang von Goethe: "Whatever you can do or dream you can, begin it. Boldness has genius, power, and magic in it." Goethe's words remind us of the transformative power of bold action.

Your Call to Action

"You win with people."—Woody Hayes.

As you embark on your journey from average to excellence—flourishing—remember that success is about personal achievement and uplifting others. By sharing your knowledge, offering support, and mentoring others, you create a cycle of growth and empowerment. Paying it forward is a winning formula.

Dream BIG by envisioning your greatest aspirations and setting ambitious goals. Step outside your comfort zone by regularly challenging yourself with new experiences and taking risks.

Delete your past mistakes and begin again. Refuse the fear. Take that next step; it may even be a great leap. Build connections with those that bring life, joy, and broader perspectives. Adjust your fixed mindset and embrace the growth mindset that we mentioned earlier.

The Global Flourishing study by Harvard's Human Flourishing program, conducted in collaboration with Gallup and other institutions, describes the impact of mindset on flourishing. This longitudinal study, with over 200,000 participants spanning twenty-two countries, showed that individuals who maintain a positive mindset are more likely to experience higher levels of flourishing.

Sixty-eight percent of those with a growth mindset reported higher life satisfaction and greater overall well-being than those with a fixed mindset. Seventy-two percent of those who actively cultivated positive habits and mindsets experienced significant improvements in their personal and professional lives.

Other research supports the impact of mindset on flourishing, showing that psychological well-being, purpose, and positive relationships also contribute. For example, gratitude and positive thinking were found to have a 40%

higher chance of flourishing, experiencing lower stress levels, and better mental health.

The journey from mediocrity to flourishing is paved with intentional actions, resilience, and a commitment to growth. As you implement these strategies, remember that your transformation will elevate not only your own life but also inspire and empower those around you.

Your journey is a testament to the boundless potential within each of us. As you strive for excellence, embrace the challenges, celebrate the victories, and always aim to impact the world positively. Rod Parsley says, "Revival starts with you." Personal transformation can spark broader change.

These principles and strategies will assist you in breaking free from the confines of mediocrity and elevating your life to one of excellence and fulfillment. Remember, the journey to fulfilling your greatest dream takes a team. Don't go alone. With each step, you are paving the way for a brighter, more extraordinary future. This is your flourishing moment... go Flourish Beyond Limits!

About Dominic Biscardi

 Visionary and forward-thinking, Dominic is a dynamic leader and executive coach renowned for building up people and businesses with a strong acumen. As a brand innovator, Dominic's highly curated teams and enterprises have garnered accolades such as *Best Place to Work and Overall Leadership.*

His unique ability to inspire and cultivate growth is evidenced by a proven track record of integrity, consistency, and empowerment marked with many recognitions. An impactful communicator and writer, Dominic weaves a narrative of success built upon a firm foundation based on solid core values.

Through a blend of strategic insight and empathetic leadership, he, along with his teams, transformed companies, setting new industry standards along the way. Known for his ability to drive innovation and foster a thriving work culture, Dominic has left an indelible mark on every organization he has been a part. His genuine approach continues to influence and motivate, making him a sought-after coach and thought leader.

To get Dominic's gift: www.LOTbook.net/gift/Dominic

For the Love of Transformation

The Joy Decision

By Christy Vermeer

I was sitting at the kitchen table when I received the phone call. "We've had a cancelation, and a spot has opened on the trip. Do you want to go?"

It was my dream—a trip to Israel—with a Master Bible teacher. He had a long waitlist, and this was my chance to go.

Except there was a catch... unlike most Israel trips, this one required me to hike 8 MILES A DAY. I had struggled with chronic physical pain for most of my life and could barely manage half a mile without crashing for days.

But I was tired of saying no to my dreams. Done with being exhausted and controlled by my pain, weighing my actions based on the amount of pain it would cost me. Missing out in moments as I watched my life go by.

I had a choice: FAITH or FEAR. I could step out in FAITH, trusting that if I put in the work, my dreams would come true. Or I could do what I'd been doing all my life. Say "no" out of FEAR and regret it for the rest of my life. I chose FAITH and started my nine-month journey preparing for that trip.

It was hard. So many days I didn't want to get out of bed and hike. It hurt too much. But then I'd tell myself, "Christy, if you don't get on that trail now, when you get to Israel, you are going to be in extreme pain and crash. You've got this, don't quit, keep moving forward. Your dream will come true."

As I got closer to the trip, I still said, "It hurts too much. I can't do this." But each time I pictured enjoying the upcoming trip, and said to myself "You've got this, don't quit, keep moving forward, your dream will come true. Keep on taking the next step."

With each step, I felt stronger and more grateful to be outside moving and feeling good. My body was learning and creating a core belief. "No matter what you feel like or how much it hurts, you can push through. You can become stronger; you can take one more step towards your dreams."

Then I was finally there, in Israel, living out my dream! The first few days were hard, but ok. On day three, I woke up hardly able to move and my first thought was, *"All that training was meaningless. I can't do this. I can't get on that bus."* Then I remembered, "You've got this, don't quit, keep moving forward, your dream will come true."

As the bus drove along the desolate Dead Sea, we headed towards the En Gedi Waterfall Oasis in the desert. I knew most tours only did a short waterfall hike, but that our group would spend the day hiking to places most people would never see.

This waterfall day was the culmination of my trip and ALL my training. It was my reason for being there. But that day, I wondered if I was strong enough? Did I have what it takes? I was in so much pain already, but I didn't want to miss it and live with regret.

It was a hot 112-degree day. People without pain were dropping like flies. Their day's journey was over. I was dizzy, dealing with heat stroke, but I would NOT quit.

In the end, only a small group of us made it to the waterfall. As I put my fingers in the water, I changed forever. I walked under the falls and as the water washed over me, everything cleared up. My strength returned, and I knew my life would never be the same as I could see a new future for myself.

I'm not saying the water miraculously healed me and my life of pain was gone. I'm saying I decided. Now I saw a happy ending to my story. I'd been on a journey, faced obstacles, and pushed through pain in route to a wondrous destination.

Realizing that if I could overcome pain, there must be a way to help others do it too. I've put that experience into a signature process I call "The Joy Decision." I joyfully spend my time giving people the skills needed to manage their pain and create a full life. To choose joy in the hardest times.

No matter the obstacle, the journey is worth taking, because there are wonderful adventures ahead.

What was the key to my success on that trip? I turned my PAIN INTO PURPOSE. We all deal with some sort of pain, and it can feel unending, overwhelming, and hopeless. I focused on the JOY in those moments and that TRANSFORMED MY LIFE.

JOY: Journey—Own It—You

J—Journey

It's about perspective. As I prepared for the trip, I kept in mind it was a journey, not a sprint. It would take training and time, but it would be worth it.

Life is a journey, and you can expect roadblocks and detours on your route. It can be tough circumstances or life hitting you with challenges you can't control. Maybe your obstacle is physical pain, mental pain, emotional pain, or even spiritual pain, but we ALL have pain.

Life is so much better when you understand there are roadblocks that slow you down, or road work throwing your life into chaos. That happens on a journey.

But do you know what also happens on a journey? You can find waterfalls, places of rest, amazing sunsets, and beautiful scenery that give your heart joy and restore your soul. On your way, you find people who are amazing friends, family, or new connections that you never had.

There will be adventures along the way, some hard and others easy. It's the contrast that gives your life meaning. After all, you can't have highs without lows, the good without the bad. Sometimes, you can't appreciate the joy without going through the pain.

That's when you learn to appreciate what you have and where you're going. If you want a more fulfilled, joyful life, stay on the journey, knowing it matters in the end.

It's also important to give yourself GRACE. Because it's not a straight line, no journey is. But your life will be richer, your life will be more blessed, and you can learn from your journey. It's up to you.

O—Own it, Own Your State

This is big. You need to OWN IT. Own it all. As I trained for the trip, I chose to be responsible for owning my personal "state" mentally, emotionally, and physically.

To succeed, I knew I needed to stop feeling sorry for myself and to stop focusing on my pain. Not only my physical pain, but this also included emotional pain from those I felt had hurt me. It wasted my energy and kept me from moving forward. I needed to focus on joy, on the good.

I decided to OWN my STATE and not let life or pain hijack it.

How do you do that? Pay attention to how you are doing, really doing. Be aware of your state, so you can change it.

1. Watch Your LANGUAGE (mental state).

It wasn't until later that I understood how much impact my language, especially my internal language, had on my success. Each time I was ready to quit, I would tell myself, "You've got this, don't quit, keep moving forward. Your dream will come true."

However, all too often, I still hurt emotionally or physically and then beat myself up with horrible words in a futile effort to stop the pain. Using negative words such as "I am so tired,

I'm in so much pain" or "It's too much. I'm not strong enough. I can't do this anymore" isn't healthy.

Your brain is amazing. You tell your brain what to look for, and it will find it. When I used negative, soul killing words, my brain confirmed it by showing all the instances of when those words were true. "Yes, you're in pain here, you're in pain there, that will cause you pain too. Don't do that, Run!"

In the same way, are you hurting yourself by consistently saying you are overwhelmed, tired, hurt, anxious, or depressed? Yes, your brain will showcase all those instances, too. Your language creates what you experience.

But you can change that by changing your words. Pay attention to your language and when you CATCH yourself saying (or thinking) something negative, SWITCH IT to something better. Remember, you can control your words.

Stop beating yourself up and turn your negative language into positive or at least less hurtful language. You could say to yourself, "I am blessed, I am grateful for, I am loved, I am purposed, I am strong and getting stronger." What a much better turn of phrase.

For example, I used to say, "My pain is killing me." Is that true? No. But your brain thinks it is, and amps up to respond to the danger.

Now, I say "It's not my best day." Does it mean the pain is gone? No. But my brain doesn't freak out and the softer language puts the pain at a lower level of importance, so I can move on with my day.

Where could you change your wording? Perhaps a situation is merely "annoying or inconvenient," instead of "destroying you" as it has done before. Better language changes how your brain responds and helps it abort the red alert your negative words have caused. Language matters.

2. Watch Your FOCUS (emotional state).

This was the hardest one to prepare for the trip. If I don't watch it, my default focus is on what's going wrong. How my pain is impeding my dreams. I learned that what I focus on is what I get. What I feel about life becomes my life.

If I tell you to look for the ways someone has been kind to you today, how many can you list? Now, if I told you to write how many times someone pissed you off instead, how many do you have? Which list is longer? Is there a pattern?

Do you see the hurt instead of the kindness? Again, your brain finds what you look for. You need to be careful in telling your brain that for which to search. Here, it's about how you feel, about the meaning you give to actions or events. Your brain will look for pain or joy. It's up to you.

I used to think of my pain as a never-ending game with no time-outs. Knowing I was headed towards destruction and unable to stop it. Now, I see life as a journey and the pain as merely an obstacle in the way.

My language has shifted, the meaning of the pain has changed. Pain no longer controls me. I have learned to dance with it instead.

Change the definition you give pain. For me, pain brings perspective, compassion, and understanding. It forces me to prioritize and say no to what wastes energy and yes to what matters most. Pain is a gift that has strengthened me—that's the meaning I choose to give it.

What about you? Is there a pain you pushed through that made you stronger? Or more grateful? Or more loving? What pain do you need to redefine or learn from in your life?

I've heard it said that "Emotion = energy in motion" and what you focus on is where your energy goes. So don't waste your energy on the pain in your life, staying stuck and hopeless. Instead, re-direct your energy towards the positive moments and people in your life. This will bring your life more joy.

3. Pay Attention to Your BODY (physical state).

For me, setting up training goals, dialing in my nutrition, and consistent hiking led to a successful trip. I prepared my body.

Physical pain is tricky. Sometimes it can be healed and other times managed. Exercise, drinking more water, watching your nutrition, and taking time to rest and refresh will strengthen your body. Listen to your body and learn what it needs to be healthier, that attention will pay off.

These three areas: your words, your focus, and your physical health combine to impact your state. If you're stuck and trying to break through, remember to own it and take charge of your state mentally, emotionally, and physically.

Y—<u>You</u>

Belief matters. Believing that I had the strength to prepare and reach for my dream trip was critical in it coming true.

It's about YOU and what you BELIEVE. Do you have a life of pain? Does everything in your life go wrong? Or do you have a life that's beautiful, amazing, fulfilling, and full of love and rich with friendships? Filled with obstacles, sure, but challenges you overcome.

You choose what you believe in and how you experience life. If you believe life is only pain—it is. If you believe life has joy—it does. Your choice.

Whatever beliefs you continually tell yourself about your life, whether it's one of pain or one of joy, become your life.

The trouble is, it's hard to have good beliefs when you're tired and hurting. Yet it's essential to get the life you want.

If you're stuck, again look for JOY. Remember, it's a journey. Give yourself GRACE. Second, manage your state so that you have the energy to create better beliefs. Third, write and consistently repeat your beliefs with positive energy until they become your life experience.

My favorite is to state them aloud while hiking or while moving to my favorite playlist. These will get you into a positive state, so that your beliefs sink in deep.

My journey to Israel and that waterfall defining moment still impacts me today. At the waterfall, my perspective shifted. For the rest of the trip, whenever it got tough, I knew I could do it, because I had done it before.

I learned that if I could just get up, I would find enough energy to take one more step and succeed. The lessons I learned on that trip I remember today, as they were burned into my body with pain. Forever reminders that life is a gift and the adventure is worth it.

I still hit bottom, but now when I do, I look for JOY and know I'll bounce back quicker because it's not about the pain, it's about loving the journey and finding the joy.

Life is too short to live in pain.

I used to struggle, feel overwhelmed or hopeless, and sometimes made decisions out of pain—whether it's from denying it, running from it, or just trying to cope. These are what I call "pain decisions."

My life changed as I looked for the JOY now, instead of the pain. I have a choice, and you do too. No matter the pain—to choose joy and transform your life forever.

The next time it's tough, I challenge you to look for the JOY. Choose Joy. Make the JOY DECISION.

About Christy Vermeer

 Christy Vermeer is a dedicated author, speaker, and Joy coach who overcame a 40-year battle with chronic pain and fatigue. Using her expertise and personal insights, she impacts the lives of many, helping them navigate the challenges of pain and reclaim their joy.

As the creator of the Joy Decision Process, Christy has developed a unique framework that helps individuals transform their mindset and embrace a life filled with purpose. Her work is centered on building hope for those who feel lost, empowering them to take back control of their lives by making everyday decisions that cultivate positivity, resilience, and hope. She encourages others to find strength in their journey.

Christy's relatable and compassionate style resonates with many, making her a sought-after speaker and coach. Her message is clear: even in the face of adversity, everyone can choose joy, and she is dedicated to sharing this message with the world.

To get Christy's gift, go to: www.LOTbook.net/gift/Christy

For the Love of Transformation

The Journey

Values Led The Way
By Alicia Becerril

Writing this chapter has been a labor of love to honor my parents, who were the salt of the earth. They made no TV appearances, had no newspaper clippings, no celebrity status. You wouldn't see them on the Oprah channel or sitting with Charlie Rose. But they lived lives and owned values that sustained goodness and decency on this earth. The values they held, and the love they gave, and the faith they embraced were the elements that comprised a life well lived. A life given to others.

Before they met, my parents, Maria and Antonio, had humble beginnings in Mexico. Before coming to the States, my mom's life was marked with loss. As an infant, she lost her mother. Her father remarried and had other children. In the fourth grade, her stepmother took only my mom out of school. Every day thereafter, she spent the day sewing pants.

She met her first husband, married, and had three beautiful children: Eva, Joe, and Victor. She was finally moving forward in life when she lost her husband to an untimely death. Thereafter, she did not have the means to feed her children. With no other options, she begged the local orphanage to care for them. For two years, she supported herself by setting up a stand and selling clothes and trinkets she made. On the weekends, she visited her children.

A distant cousin visited Guadalajara and discovered my mother's plight. She invited my mom and the kids to live with her in Sacramento, California. There, she found work at an almond factory. These early losses were a crucible in which my mom shaped and framed a life for herself and her soon-to-be growing family.

My dad, papi, also lost his mother when he was very young. He was born in Aparo, Michoacan, a town reachable only by train. The town had dirt streets, and the scanty houses had no flooring, only dirt. I once visited and remember a chicken flying through a window into my dad's family house.

My father was pulled out of school after the third grade. At 14, he left his home to live and work with an older brother in Mexico City. At 19, he went to Chicago, Illinois, to work as a bracero where he worked with a railroad company.

After returning to Aparo, he could not find work. He decided to look for work in the States. He taught himself English by staying in his bedroom for three months and listening to a language record! Then he traveled to Sacramento, California, where he again found work with the railroad.

There, at the age of 20, he met my mom. She was 7 years older with three children. They fell in love and married, and as good Catholics, raised five more children: Mary Ellen. Terri, Alicia, Juanita, David, and Linda.

My dad later worked as a cabinetmaker with Ray Corum who opened doors for my father. On some weekends, Mr. Corum invited our family to join him and his family to enjoy water skiing in the summer and snow skiing in the winter. My dad wanted these experiences for his kids so he bought a motorboat, water skis and snow ski equipment (all second hand). We were a bit on the raggedy side, but this posed no deterrence.

Mr. Corum became a residential developer and built homes in a good neighborhood. My father joined him in that venture. Prior to this, he took correspondence courses to earn his high school equivalence degree and a general contractor's license. In that residential development, my dad built the house we later lived in.

My dad loved telling jokes and making people laugh. He worked hard and expected to have dinner on the table when he got home. He could be gruff and impatient. I was, at times, shy in talking with him. However, as I grew older, I became bolder and learned to engage in lively conversations with him at the dinner table. He read Newsweek and the local newspaper. We loved to talk about politics and the issues of the day. Also, although I was sometimes half-asleep, I enjoyed talking with him to ensure he stayed awake during the several day and sometimes all night travel to Mexico City in a station wagon filled with kids.

My parents often spoke about the importance of education. My mom spoke only Spanish but encouraged our English at home. She insisted that we be educated. If you had homework, that would trump chores, like washing dishes. So, I made sure I always had homework!

My mom taught us hard work. While she was a great believer in being on your knees when you prayed, she also believed in being on your knees when you worked. Every Saturday, we would polish the dining and living room hardwood floors on our knees. And believe me, I prayed for Sunday to come!

On Sundays, my parents devoted the day to us. After mass, we had menudo or hot cakes. In the afternoon, we would go to the park or watch a movie. On the days we went skiing, my mom would pack a feast, including her legendary tortillas.

From the loss of her mother, my mom became a mom's mom, treasuring us children, looking for ways to offer us goodies even as we sometimes struggled. She found ways. Wonder bread with real butter was quite the treat.

My mom nurtured us and stressed that good health was a wondrous blessing. She would often say that if you have your health, you have everything. She looked for healthy ways to eat, and that led to breakfasts of liver, onions, and orange juice! One time I refused to eat my lima beans at dinner. I had to sit at the kitchen table until dark. She enforced the veggie law!

While she nurtured us in all these ways, she also nurtured her garden. It was impeccably laid out. Gardening was her way of finding peace and relaxation.

My mom nurtured family, flowers, and her faith as well. She was devoted to the church, especially the Our Lady of Guadalupe Church. She was a Guadalupana. In later years, her cooking expertise came into play. Every Saturday, she joined the Guadalupanas in making tamales to sell on Sundays to support the church.

She was also a master at sewing. When we were young, my three sisters and I often looked like quadruplets, wearing the same dress our mom made for each of us.

My mom loved singing, swimming, and playing the guitar. She was active and didn't enjoy sitting around. She was steeped in self-reliance and passed that value along to us. My mom left us a legacy of service, serenity, and peace. We would do well to heed her advice: Study, eat your veggies, work hard, serve the community, and love the Lord and His Mother.

She loved her travels with her first-born Eva to Rome and Jerusalem. For a short period, she lived with David near Seattle, Washington. Watching the chickens cackling away in the backyard beat anything on TV.

My mom took her faith seriously in her everyday life. She hated gossip. She loved the rosary. Let's face it. She'd have been an extraordinarily dedicated nun. Only eight children stood in her way!

She prayed for her children without ceasing, including during the fatal illness of my sister Juanita. At the age of six, when I was seven, Juanita became ill with leukemia. My parents spent several weeks at the hospital before she passed. Her loss was devastating to each of us. I lost my best friend.

During that same year, I chipped my front tooth twice. Then our dog bit me on the face as I attempted to pet him. I was unaware that he was chewing on a bone. The result was nine stitches and a large scar. My older sister said, "No one will want to marry her now." Sometimes I was called "ugly" so I knew I couldn't depend on my looks. Instead, I turned to reading books and getting good grades.

A year later, my father's only biological son, David, was born. The good news was that my father gave him a lot of attention. The bad news was that my father gave him a lot of attention. In our culture, boys are of prime importance. My dad was enormously proud of him and had high expectations of him. He actively shaped my brother's baseball skills as his coach and manager.

In our house, David was not allowed in the kitchen to cook. Rather, his job was to mow the lawn or to perform other outside chores.

During one summer, he was an exchange student in Finland. There, he learned to cook vegetarian meals and to sew a kaftan. When he came home, David often cooked his own meals and sometimes wore the kaftan. My dad could only grumble.

After becoming a physician, David and his family traveled to Mexico to provide medical services through the program

Time for Christ. Today, David is a physician in Washington. There, he practices family medicine and tends to the Spanish-speaking community. He also volunteers for a homeless shelter clinic. He swims or runs every day. He and his wife Monica have fun cooking feasts and watching cooking shows. Two of his children, Jordan and Alissa, also became physicians and are talented musicians.

When David was two, my sister Linda was born. However, I had no idea my mom was pregnant. She wore loose clothing and kept doing her chores. Then one day, she was at the hospital. My dad was somber when he returned from the hospital. I asked him what the baby's name was. He did not answer. Not long after, Linda became the favorite.

My dad was a handyman at work and at home. Linda loved to follow him as he made his way around the house, fixing things. While traipsing after him, she wore a play tool kit around her waist. It was adorable. To this day, Linda is a whiz at fixing things and working on projects.

Mary Ellen, a surgical nurse, was a treasure. She was always there for my dad, and always there for the rest of us. She lived in Stockton with her husband, Al, and son, Freddy. Without fail, she joined us for Sunday dinner and other special occasions. Any time I had an ailment, she gave me sisterly medical advice. She made me feel like she was my biggest fan. Amazingly, she made each of us feel that way.

In later years, my dad suffered from pancreatic cancer. During his illness, Mary Ellen was by his side every day. She continued to travel to and from Stockton to work and care for my dad. Linda also made caring for my dad a priority.

After four months, my dad passed away. He was surrounded by love and tenderness. Before he became ill, he said that if he died at that moment, he would die a happy man. He loved his daughters, and his daughters loved him.

In her late 50s, Mary Ellen contracted breast cancer. She underwent chemotherapy and was in remission for seven years. Then the cancer returned. She again started chemotherapy. During that period, I had planned to travel to Assisi with my dear friend, Angela Alioto, a civil rights attorney and politician in San Francisco. My sister surprised me by asking if she and her husband could join us. Angela graciously welcomed them.

Angela is beyond knowledgeable on anything relating to Francesco (St. Francis). She gave my sister and her husband a personal tour of Francesco's favorite places. We walked for long distances. We complained about how tired we were and how sore our feet were. Though the after-effects of the chemotherapy caused severe pain to my sister's feet, she said nothing. She was simply happy to be there.

Within a few months thereafter, as Mary Ellen was dying, she expressed her wishes for her son, and also said, "I love Angela, and I love St. Francis." She wanted Angela do her eulogy. On her last night with us, we all gathered around her as my mom prayed the rosary. We were heartbroken. Amazingly, my mom was the one who comforted us. Angela fulfilled my sister's request at a special ceremony at the National Shrine of St. Francis in San Francisco.

Speaking of Assisi, I first visited there over twenty years ago. Immediately, I felt how sacred and special it was. Visually, at every turn, I saw picture-perfect beauty. During that visit, I was a member of the San Francisco Board of Supervisors. With a letter from Mayor Willie Brown in hand, I received a warm welcome. The Chief of police gave me a tour of the city.

In the afternoon, I received a walking tour of the little shops. It was a day I shall always remember. Every year since then, I have traveled back to Assisi and other towns in Italy.

Years later, Angela spearheaded a movement to build a replica of the Porziuncola here in San Francisco. The Porziuncola was the chapel that Francesco rebuilt and was his favorite place in the world. Although taking photos and measurements was strictly prohibited, Angela brought a group of us to measure it. Our measurements with dental floss were off by only 1/6 of an inch.

However, we did not go unnoticed. The next day, the Provential Minister, Massimo Rasiglian, called Angela into his office. He asked who gave her the authority to take measurements. She pointed upwards. After a four-hour discussion, he gave Angela permission to build a replica in San Francisco, including full access to the chapel for photos and measurements on a selected day. The Porziuncola Nuova is now a gem in San Francisco.

Getting back to my parents, throughout their journey, and in spite of the loss of their youth, my parents ensured that we children had full access to the adventures of childhood, including the boat for waterskiing, the car trips to Mexico, and the drives to go snow skiing.

From the loss of their education, my parents instilled in us the primacy of going to school and advancing. And we did. My siblings each used their education to go into different careers. David is a physician. I am a lawyer and administrative law judge; my son Alex is a lawyer. Linda was a court reporter. Mary Ellen was a surgical nurse. Joe worked as a jet technician and entrepreneur. Eva, Terri, and Victor worked as computer operators; each was creative and bright.

Over 25 years of higher education were affirmed and supported by parents who didn't go beyond grade school. They believed in the possibility of a better life for themselves and for their children. Similarly, we owe it to our children to offer them the steppingstones to a better life.

About Alicia Becerril

 Alicia Becerril is a dedicated legal consultant specializing in employment law, offering invaluable guidance to employers navigating complex legal landscapes. With a J.D. degree from the University of California at Davis School of Law, Alicia combines her extensive academic background with practical experience to provide comprehensive legal advice tailored to her clients' needs.

Alicia's distinguished career includes serving as a former adjunct law professor, litigation attorney in personal injury and commercial business cases, and an administrative law judge. Her unique blend of legal expertise and public service experience positions her as a trusted advisor for organizations seeking to foster fair and equitable workplace practices.

Alicia Becerril is known for her integrity, professionalism, and dedication to empowering employers and workers to reach resolutions prior to litigation. Through her work, she continues to make a positive impact on the legal landscape and the organizations she serves.

To get Alicia's gift, go to: www.LOTbook.net/gift/Alicia

For the Love of Transformation

Falling in Love with the Path

By Kathleen Jones

I spent much of my life on *a path I thought I should follow.*

Perhaps you can relate. You might find yourself living someone else's expectation of who you should be, unable to see your unique gifts, or underestimating yourself and what's possible.

The word *"follow"* is also key here, because when you're on your own path, you're not *following* it, you are *forging* it. It becomes uniquely your own, a path of self-discovery as you become more brilliant and more fully *yourself.*

In her book, *Living Your Top Five Percent*, Jennifer Caragol, MD, describes engaging your innate strengths to their fullest.

"These superpowers, seeded in you from birth, spring from your true nature. They are your resources, power, and gifts for this lifetime. Only you have this array of qualities, and when you put these qualities in service to your mission, they are your soul in action. Then you bring something wondrous into the world — *something only you can create.*"

This discovery and understanding — that you can activate your strengths, align with your vision, and live into your potential — has been a driving force in my work as a coach, mentor, and trainer.

It's what led me to attend a live event with world class trainer and voice coach Roger Love. From the moment he stepped onstage, he was riveting, playful, and provocative. He showed how you and I can *choose how we sound*. I discovered I could bring more emotion and more edge to my voice; I could vary the pacing and the pitch. The techniques I learned from him helped me reach new levels in my career: creating courses through Embody Change Coaching, landing speaking engagements and teaching opportunities, writing, and recording a series of guided mindfulness sessions with eMindful.

And something else unexpected surfaced in that live event — a glimpse of a path I'd once traveled, a path that had become overgrown and barely visible.

Decades before, I'd written and recorded songs but dismissed them as not good enough. I believed my voice wasn't strong enough; that I was too old to play in a rock band. I was terrified on stage. But somewhere buried in all the self-doubt was a tiny spark of possibility.

Maybe you've had that experience, a moment in which you rediscover a part of yourself that's been left behind or forgotten.

Arriving home, I listened to the recordings I'd made years ago, an experience that was powerful beyond words. The songs felt evocative and magical; my voice gave me chills. Listening to those recordings was like falling into a time warp or into a dream state, evoking not only the recollection of *who I once was*, but also recognizing the creative spark still within me — and a glimpse of what the future might hold.

I relearned songs I'd written and began writing new songs. I found the courage to reach out to a bass player and connect with my former drummer, to form a band that has taken on a life of its own: playing shows and festivals, recording songs, and getting steady radio play in the US, in Canada, and in Sweden. We were signed to an independent label and nominated for a grammy in the category of best rock song.

To the outside world, transformation can look like magic. Those around you may be surprised and even amazed while the genuine change — the source of it all — is happening at the core of your being. This *inner transformation* allows you to see yourself in a new light, to go beyond ego and self-judgment, to be receptive and playful and to step into a shimmering field of creative freedom.

This, my friend, is my wish for you: that you may connect with, align with, and light up the path that is calling you.

In that spirit, I share with you a few thoughts to help guide you along whatever path you choose.

Beginning with the question, *What kind of transformation do you want to bring about?*

Maybe it's reclaiming a part of yourself to find the work you love or feel more vibrant or creatively alive. Getting clear on what you want provides direction, but that alone won't get you there. Forward movement requires taking steps; it requires that you travel the path.

In the pages ahead, you'll explore how you can clarify your vision and forge a transformative path that is uniquely yours... *and* fall in love with the path itself.

First, I invite you to realize ALL that you are; to know that you possess a vast reservoir of potential, far beyond what you can see.

You are the sculptor, author, and director of your own life. You can go beyond simply inhabiting your former life — or the life you think you should be living — to embrace what's emerging and most alive for you. Tap into the vital force within known as *élan vitale*.

Whatever you have in mind, you CAN make it happen.

Your Vision

> *INTENTION pulls us moment to moment, hence the importance of being clear.*
>
> -Maetzumi Roshi

Knowing what you want is not always easy. When I ask coaching clients what they want for themselves, they often respond with, "I don't know." They mention things they ought to do, like finishing their degree, even though their heart isn't in it.

If your vision is hazy, trust that it will develop as you move forward. The vision and the path are not linear... they flow into and feed one another.

Sometimes transformation begins with a growing sense of *discontent* — uncertain of what you want, but knowing that this is not it. Earlier in my career, teaching in a family medicine training program had become the core of my professional identity—even as I sensed that it no longer aligned with my true calling. Those around me questioned why on earth I'd want to leave an esteemed faculty position? Logically, it made no sense.

Friends and family members sometimes discourage you because they see only the risk, or they know you based on who you've been rather than who you are *becoming*, or they can't see the possibilities ahead and therefore can't cheer you on until after you've arrived.

If you're uncertain, you might ask yourself what you're most drawn to and when and where you feel most alive. You might imagine your perfect day: what you're doing, whom you're with, and the emotions you feel: exhilaration... a sense of wonder or challenge... joy... a heartfelt connection with others...

The emotional experience is critical because without it, your vision will feel lifeless and flat. It won't have the emotional charge needed to inspire and activate change.

The last line of my mission statement is, *"step to the edge, sometimes falling."* The sense of standing at the edge of a cliff evokes both terror and exhilaration. It has an emotional charge that motivates and reminds me to lean into new experiences—and to accept that at times I *will* fall.

Words and images can be powerful reminders of your intentions. Perhaps you have your own mission statement or vision board, or a tattoo that reminds you of your intention to take risks or to be kind or whatever it might be.

The word "vision" usually suggests the *outcome*: "To lead a retreat near the ocean," but we can also envision *how we will arrive there*. If your vision is to showcase your paintings in an artsy cafe, you might imagine the paintings hanging in the space — and see yourself at work in your studio, noticing the play of light, the texture of the paint, the movement of the brush...

Despite the language, this practice isn't limited to the visual realm. It's most potent when you engage all of your senses, leaning into the emotions and the *felt experience*: the butterflies or sense of awe or accomplishment.

The poet Rilke wrote that *"the future must enter you long before it happens."* Visioning forges new neural pathways, laying down *future memories*, giving you the sense that you've already been there. The path feels familiar, as if some part of you has traveled ahead and is waiting for you to arrive.

If you find it challenging to imagine the future, you might instead evoke a time in the past when you *were* confident or creative, or when you felt excited and fully alive, bringing *that* into your conscious awareness and pulling it into the here and now. It's how I found my way back to songwriting: reconnecting with and *reclaiming* who I once was and

144

bringing it into the present moment — which then became the basis for envisioning and engaging with the path ahead.

The Path

The path comprises the thoughts, emotions, and actions that lead to the change(s) you want to create.

If you want to feel more at ease in your body, the path might involve regular yoga practice. If you want to advance in your career, it might mean reading books and working toward a certificate in your field. Or, if you want to be more present and joyful, it might involve paying attention to and appreciating the good that comes your way.

Some actions are single steps — like buying new running shoes or signing up for a class — whereas others are daily practices. There is immense power in daily practice, in part because *consistent action leads to results*. THAT leads to transformation.

Consistent practice builds habits. This is key because once an action becomes a habit, it no longer requires much motivation or willpower. You no longer need to decide whether to work out or study or whatever it might be. Like putting on a seatbelt, it becomes something you do with little thought.

As William James wrote more than a century ago: "We must make automatic and habitual, as early as possible, as many useful actions as we can." When we do this, "our higher powers of mind will be set free for their own proper work."

It helps to begin with something so small that you cannot fail, beginning with *micro-practice*, like writing for one minute every day — and growing the practice.

It also helps to build *ritual* into your practice. To eat more mindfully, you could create a beautiful place setting, sit upright in your chair, and offer an expression of gratitude — elevating your experience with intention and inspiration.

"What is a daily practice? It is a way that you take your existence seriously, one breath at a time, one thought at a time, one moment at a time. It is your daily routine of paying attention to the areas where you have set your intentions. It looks like the silence of deep space filled with the brilliant fire of a single star. It is you spending a significant amount of time every day focused in one direction."

-Eric Maisel

Falling in Love With the Path

Virya is a Sanskrit word that translates as *joyful perseverance*; effort imbued with wisdom and joy; an attitude in which we are enthusiastically engaged at every step along the way.

I recently heard Norman Fischer describe it in this way:

"Yes, we have a goal in mind or an outcome in mind. But when we focus our energy on that outcome and see our effort as simply a slog through to get to that outcome, we lose our way. What matters is the effort itself, not the goal. The goal is direction. The joy is in the path, walking toward that direction."

146

"Don't move the way fear makes you move. Move the way love makes you move. Move the way joy makes you move."
- Osho

I'll offer a couple of examples of how virya shows up in my life:

One of my core practices is playing guitar most evenings. Sometimes I play for an hour or more, other times for just a few minutes. In that time, I let go of whatever else I should (or could) be doing to enter a joy-filled and receptive flow state — the wellspring of creative inspiration.

Now, you might be thinking that it's easy to fall in love with a practice that is enjoyable — *playing* music. Absolutely true... so here's another example on the other end of the pleasure spectrum...

I recently moved into a new space. Ordinarily I'd focus on the difficulty and disruption of moving, but because I'd just listened to the interview with Norman Fischer, I was inspired to approach it as joyfully as possible. I mindfully packed and gave items away, and on the other side, I unpacked each box *as if opening a gift*, with heartfelt gratitude.

We can find joy on the path, embrace the process itself, and live the *in-between moments* of our lives with greater presence and grace.

I hope this chapter will inspire you to live all the moments of life fully, to believe in yourself, and to trust that a well-chosen path *will* lead to transformation.

The practices and the path begin as something you *do* and, over time, become *part of who you are*. You come to think of yourself as an artist... a leader... a writer... a force for good... as someone who is confident and self-assured. External validation is no longer needed as you come to realize ALL that you are.

I wish you immense love and joy along whatever path you call your own.

Listen to Serpentine at:
https://www.youtube.com/watch?v=Fb2eluhDo38

About Kathleen Jones

As a coach, mentor, trainer, and writer Kathleen Jones brings extensive experience and depth to the field of personal transformation.

Founder of Embody Change Coaching, she trains aspiring and established coaches, creating and offering several nationally accredited courses including *Exploring the Landscape of Emotions, Creating Goals that Come Alive* and *Coaching Toward High-Level Performance.*

For over two decades, she taught behavior change, lifestyle medicine, and spirituality in medicine to family medicine resident physicians.

She's taught yoga and mindfulness in multiple settings, including writing daily mindfulness meditations for eMindful.

Kathleen skillfully weaves together mind-body awareness with a solid understanding of how to elicit positive change. She invites clients and students to go deep within themselves, calling forth their own inner wisdom and strengths to create inspired and lasting change.

Living next to a mountain park in Colorado, Kathleen enjoys hiking, time with friends and family, and is the lead singer and songwriter in the psychedelic rock band Serpentine.

To get Kathleen's gift: www.LOTbook.net/gift/Kathleen

For the Love of Transformation

Discovering the Path to your Superpowers

By Lisa Gray

What if I told you there were some techniques you could try that might help you discover how to better accomplish your goals? Techniques that can explain why Plan A works for some people, but doesn't seem to work for you, or why Plan B made you worse. If this resonates with you, please keep reading.

Being a lifelong learner is an integral part of who I am. Sometimes I think it's because I love to learn, or I think it's because I didn't seem to fit into mainstream ways of thinking. Honestly, I do not know. However, I value people's set of unique skills that I am calling superpowers.

This became crystal clear to me when I took classes to become an EMT. Both the instruction and hands on practice were great. However, the standardized test was the single hardest test I have ever taken, and this was after college. This was 40 years ago and still has left an impression.

Turning the required knowledge into a standardized test may have been the problem. However, the way the questions worked was quite complex. There was a brief description of a scene followed by a question asking what actions should be taken. The answers comprised a series of letters. Each letter corresponded to an action.

The answers offered were different in both the choice of tasks and the order in which to do them. While I understand the reason for the questions and knowledge is important, it does not compare to seeing it in person. The skills needed for the job are quite different.

My point in giving you this detail is that if I were in an accident, I would NOT want to see me (a good test taker) at my window, I would want one of those experienced responders who can remain calm, quickly assess, and act. Experience is a brilliant teacher. Some qualities are hard to evaluate and even harder to see in a "standardized" way.

I do not believe there is a one-size that fits all. While people have much in common, we are all unique. This can be amazing, and it can be frustrating. Many of my bodywork clients have found their way to me after being frustrated by Western medicine, for example. If there was one-size or one path or one plan that worked for everyone, then everyone would be fit, healthy, lean, mean, well-oiled machines... or something like that, right?

One of these areas where people are similar, but different, is in processing styles. Everyone has visual, auditory, and kinesthetic abilities, but the order of preference is individual. Personally, I am kinesthetic first, visual second, and auditory last. This order supported my abilities to work with a wide variety of clients, in any setting, as an Occupational Therapist, Registered (OTR). I could more easily pick up non-verbal cues or connect with clients who were challenged by verbal communication.

It was the paperwork that had me rethinking my profession. Documenting treatment notes and writing for insurance reimbursement became frustrating for me, while some of my coworkers seemed to have a much easier time. All jobs have the details, hoops, and frustrations along with the fun stuff. The difference is in what tasks come easier and which are more challenging for an individual.

What do you think your order would be? Are you visual or auditory first? Which channel is the last for you? Do you match with friends or coworkers? How about the people who don't seem to "get" you? Understanding this can explain some differences in your processes. While society or some majority place value on certain qualities, I appreciate differences and your unique set of superpowers.

Even writing this chapter, I was given a new technique to try. I was excited because I've wanted to write for a long time. Of course I tried the process, and I didn't get the results I was expecting. Then I tried again each day. I'm better at stopping before I get too frustrated. One day, the sixth, I woke up early with my head full of words. I grabbed my notebook and a pen and dumped it all out. That was 80% of my chapter. An earlier version of me might have given up.

There were many reasons I chose the continuing education that I did. Looking at it now, it may seem an odd mix. I often learned something unexpected and sometimes something about myself along the way. I studied cranial sacral therapy, therapeutic massage, zero balancing, visceral manipulation; the list continues. Once I became a structural integrator, that became my main foundation for all the other teaching to complement.

When I enrolled in Tom Myers's first certification class for structural integration, I learned a new way of seeing the body and its structure. That was in 1999. This entire chapter is based on my current view of what I have experienced, learned, and have taken away from many wonderful teachers.

I learned our bodies are built more like a suspension bridge than a stack of blocks. Our bones are framework and spacers that protect our organs and are moved by soft tissue. The nerves and blood vessels follow a highway-like path dividing into main roads and side streets. Injury, inflammation, and lack of motion, among other things, can cause scarring or stickiness that hinders the natural slide and glide of these parts. It also limits the delivery of supplies and the removal of waste, which can contribute to difficulty with clean up and repair, also known as healing.

After spending years with the goals of helping people be in less pain, move better, and accomplish more of what they want to do, I appreciate our body's wisdom. When I am working with a client, I am tapping into that wisdom, or at least that's what it feels like, because I don't decide where to start. Also, that place may not be one part the client identified as a problem. Where I start makes sense to my client as I work. Creating some slack gives me the space to help unravel or unknot a strain pattern.

It reminds me of someone knitting or crocheting. If a knot forms in the yarn, the knot needs to be undone to continue making the project. Cutting it out will not make a good result. However, creating space and unwinding the knot allows the person to wrap the yarn back up into a smooth ball, allowing them to resume their project.

Our soft tissue and fascia suspend our skeleton. Where there are "knots" or tight places, this system becomes challenged or uncomfortable. Curiously, where it hurts is not always where the problem is. It often feels like undoing those yarn knots. There are models of tensegrity that use sticks and rubber bands to make a 3D structure. In this model, the sticks do not touch each other: they are suspended by the rubber bands. If one grabs some of those rubber bands and pulls or twists them, the shape changes and often the sticks touch.

Returning to the idea that one-size does not fit all and where it hurts may not be where the problem originates from, how does one navigate a structure as complicated as the body?

I listen to my clients' bodies because, in my experience, their body knows best. Is there a way that an individual can help themselves? I believe there is. For me, learning to navigate included being able to tune into my structure first.

One exercise I learned from Irene Lyon, taking her 21-day nervous system reset course, was to tap into the awareness of three things: gravity, breathing, and the environment. This was the first class that I took after my office was closed at the start of the lockdown because of Covid. I practiced often and noticed emotions coming up.

Fortunately, I knew all I needed to do was greet or welcome them, like a guest, and they would move on. Unwanted emotions can be stored: acknowledging them calmly allows them to continue their way without getting stuck. Things can come into our bodies, be stored, and be released. These "things" can include emotions and pain, but with this exercise, there is no need to relive or analyze this process.

There are many places to learn about breathing to become calmer. Many of these increase my anxiety. Having a longer exhale than inhaling helps. No counting, no judging, I keep going even if I'm not doing it every breath.

Another important concept for me was about the 3Bs from Ron Murray, D.O. He is an osteopath who taught several of my continuing education courses about bodywork. He put forward the idea of ways of thinking, schools of thought, and professions. All of which have the three B's: Brilliance, Blind Spots, and Bias. I had never considered this before. When being taught something, there is often an assumed understanding that what is being taught is factual.

Some math courses seem more concretely based on facts. However, I remember thinking that data could be presented in different ways depending on the process used in statistics. For example, one can find articles quoting research about something and the conclusions often sound factual. Then I remember that one of my supervisors made a comment about research on sensory integration that went something like, "You could turn trucks around in the holes of the research."

Without understanding a topic, it is easy to take information at face value. While one can see some positive outcomes in a type of treatment, for example, it can frustrate trying to prove it. One reason is that people are vastly different. For research to be sound, the sample size needs to be large. In studying people, maintaining the integrity of the study seems unrealistic. While the idea of pure, unbiased, study of a topic may sound ideal, most studies are driven by something else. Realities of needing funding, or the limits of what can realistically or ethically be studied, can get tangled with the ideal.

While most people are knowledgeable about many topics, it doesn't seem likely to say that people are knowledgeable about all topics. Even with topics that I have knowledge about, I can be swayed if I am not careful. That knowledge made the idea of the 3Bs a total game changer. There are many, many places where one assumes the expert knows best, doctors, lawyers, CEOs, moms, dads, religious leaders, political leaders, business leaders, and so on.

When you break it down, you can see where they may have a bias based on their frame of reference; their assumptions and experiences are great examples. Western medicine has testing, diagnosis, surgery, and medication in their toolbox. These tools may be a source of brilliance, as well as the origin of bias.

Brilliance is much easier to see whether it is a successful treatment via surgery, medication, casting, rehab, or many other examples. The bias can show up when a test doesn't show a problem, or a person does not respond well to a medication. What was assumed; what was missed? Some people have great success with an alternative treatment, an idea that was perhaps in a western medicine blind spot.

I have found that the 3B's idea helps me to broaden my focus. I don't put things in a good or bad category; instead, I note what seems to work well, what seems to miss, and I look for what is not being considered.

My personal struggles and challenges, coupled with trial and error, taught me that our bodies have wisdom. It isn't always easy, but I do much better when I listen. There was a "ground and fill" exercise that was introduced to me by Suzanne Scurlock, for example. This idea was like some other guided meditations I have heard. However, this method was easy to learn and effective for me.

There are many types, or schools of thought, when thinking about this type of practice. I struggled with practices that seemed to focus on length and/or consistency. Finding any technique that helps an individual to slow down, listen to their body and is adaptable to time seems to work for many people, including myself. When I run across a technique that resonates, but is hard to put into practice, I try to adapt it.

When working with people, especially in a hands-on way like a body worker, creating a boundary or a bubble of some kind is necessary. It can be quite easy to kind of "vacuum" people while working on a client's issue by taking things from the client into their own body. I even did this as an OTR without realizing it. When talking about how it can be draining working with people, we described it like wearing a vest of Velcro and the "stuff" being small Velcro covered balls.

My peers told me not to pick up other people's stuff. As I thought about it, I said I didn't actively do that. It was more like I walked into the room and the balls just flew to my vest and stick. They took this in stride, which I am grateful for every day, and they told me I needed to give them back because they weren't mine. To imagine peeling them off and returning them didn't sit well with me. We agreed that if I peeled them off, setting them on the floor would be good enough.

While in massage school, this same topic came up. It isn't healthy to see clients with pain, and have the therapist go home feeling similar pain (the vacuum idea). There was discussion among us about ways to handle this. Things like visualizing handcuffs on the therapist or wearing a non-stick coat. Ironically, it was my mother-in-law who honed my ability to do this. I found that if I pictured a soap bubble (tough, not pop-able) around me, with a vent to let in anything I needed, that worked. If I used a hard, non-stick surface, she would "bang on it" until I was exhausted.

Being able to decide how, when, or why I want to use a self-care technique has been freeing for me. It is part of making it my own and not conforming to the one-size fits all methods that frustrate me. I will say that until I practice with some diligence, like I did with the writing exercise, I won't know if or how a technique might work for me. It's very easy to give up too early. Being able to listen to my body makes progress much easier. It's not perfect, but the more I listen and heed what I hear, the clearer and faster the information comes.

The other piece of the puzzle is to look at where the assumptions I make based on media, opinion, and schools of thought may not fit what is true for me. There are often several points of view that, when revealed, make the path forward much clearer.

About Lisa J. Gray

Lisa J. Gray, she/her, is a seasoned therapist with over 40 years of experience in occupational therapy, structural integration, and bodywork. A graduate of Quinnipiac College, Lisa earned her Bachelor of Science degree in Occupational Therapy, which laid the foundation for her career dedicated to enhancing the well-being of her clients. She opened her private practice, BodyOasis, in 1999.

Lisa's holistic approach combines evidence-based techniques with personalized care, ensuring that each client receives tailored treatment that addresses their unique needs and goals. She is committed to empowering her clients to take charge of their health and well-being, providing them with the tools and strategies necessary for long-lasting improvement. As a lifelong learner, Lisa continues to add knowledge, skills, and techniques to her sessions.

Lisa's experience enables her to address a wide range of physical concerns, from chronic pain and mobility issues to athletic performance enhancement. She also enjoys attending continuing education as a student, as an assistant, or as a member of staff.

To get Lisa's gift, go to: www.LOTbook.net/gift/Lisa

For the Love of Transformation

Passion, Purpose, and Power

Let the Samurai Strategist Be Your Guide

By Lori Tsugawa

I grew up on a berry farm in rural southwest Washington State after World War II. As a third-generation Japanese American, my parents taught our family the value of hard work and determination by laboring on the farm. Although I did not particularly care for my circumstances, it taught me many lessons which would become the basis for understanding and appreciating my rich heritage.

Most of my classmates had never seen an Asian person, so I was somewhat of an oddity, an object of ridicule, bullying, and scorn. I just wanted to look like my classmates to avoid the shame—but I could not change the way I looked.

My parents emphasized hard work, determination, and bringing honor to the family and the Japanese American community. World War II was still fresh in people's minds, and we had to prove that we were good citizens who could be trusted.

I was blamed for the bombing of Pearl Harbor, a heavy burden for young shoulders. However, there was something inside that would not allow the pain to defeat me.

In school, I was an honor student, cheerleader, and enjoyed an active social life. Later, in college, I studied Japanese for the language requirement. I wanted to understand the "secret code" my parents used to communicate with each other!

After graduating with a BA in Art, I was employed by the Tacoma Art Museum as assistant to the curator, Sara Little. She was an international designer and encouraged me to travel to Japan so I would understand my roots. Sara had worked in Japan and became a positive influence in my life even to this day.

My husband and I traveled to Japan in 1982 and met my father's relatives. It changed my life! There were so many family similarities, even their sense of humor and laughter. They gave us a copy of our Tsugawa family tree and our family crest. I did not realize the significance of the crest until later in life.

After Japan, we moved to the country and were blessed to find a Japanese-style home! We raised our two sons, and it was a busy time. They grew up so quickly.

In 2005 and again in 2007, I was in rear-end car accidents. After the second incident in 2007, I noticed that something was different. I was diagnosed with mild traumatic brain injury (TBI). I also suffered chronic pain, cognitive deficits, and was reading at a seventh-grade level.

Earlier in my life I had developed a deep aversion to doctors. Now I had to face my fear because it was imperative to seek medical care to help me improve. Gradually I achieved a path of healing recovery though it took many years and hundreds of appointments.

During the time of recovery, fortitude and perseverance were paramount. I was determined to overcome TBI and believed if I could author a book, I would. Drawn to my Japanese heritage, every day I researched and wrote, even if it was only for 15 minutes. The Samurai warriors intrigued me, and I began reading about their culture and history. They lived by a moral code, Bushido, the Way of the Warrior. One day as I was researching, I recognized our family crest. I discovered our family was of Samurai lineage. What appeared to be hearts and funny shaped triangles were a unique design symbolizing a Samurai bloodline. I knew then that the DNA of the samurai warrior was in me! As my research and writing continued, my condition improved. Finally, after a herculean effort, the book was sent to the printer. In 2015, the initial shipment of books arrived on my front porch, and I thought, "YES" the DNA of the Samurai warrior really is in me!

Tsugawa *Kamon* (Family Crest)

Once the book was completed, Toastmasters helped me maintain my recovery. As my topic, I often spoke about Bushido, with its moral code of ethics which includes courage, integrity, benevolence, respect, honesty, honor, and loyalty. The Samurai pledged their lives and sacred honor to uphold this code. Bushido permeated Japanese society; the affects are still evident today.

What I learned about the foundational concepts of my heritage impacted me in such a profound way, I believe they should be shared to help our world.

My mission has become sharing and teaching the Japanese concepts of the Code of Bushido, Ikigai, and Ganbaru to help overcome life's challenges.

- Code of Bushido—武士道, "the Way of the Warrior" is the moral code which includes courage, integrity, benevolence, respect, honesty, honor, and loyalty.
- Ikigai—"iki" 生き, which means "life," and "gai" 甲斐, refers to value or worth —finding your purpose in life.
- Ganbaru—頑張, means never give up, stand firm, and follow through to completion.

Bushido

Bushido is the moral framework. Principles of courage, integrity, honesty, and honor encourage us to strive for high moral ground regardless of the circumstances. Good morals never go out of style.

Take for example, Chiune Sugihara, the Japanese vice consul in Kaunas, Lithuania, during World War II. Confronted with Jewish refugees trying to escape Nazi annihilation, he chose to help save their lives. Disobeying his government, he wrote and provided transit visas that saved an estimated 6,000 lives. This courageous act cost him his career, yet in his heart of hearts, he knew he did the right thing. His example shows us how Bushido's principles provide the bulwark for overcoming challenges, even in tough times.

In Japan, lessons are taught by example, and community. Honesty is instilled early on when a child first visits the police station to return a "found" coin. They learn to return items not belonging to themselves and the police are seen as nonthreatening and helpful.

Personally, I have experienced Japanese honesty when I left packages behind at a market and returned to find them untouched. I feel safe in Japan and can walk the streets of Kyoto solo even at night. Additionally, children can be seen riding public transportation and walking without adult supervision; an amazing testament in this day!

Ikigai

Ikigai is a way for a person to determine their purpose in life. Based on an ancient concept from Okinawa, it integrates one's passion and skills with what the world needs and is willing to pay for. The overlap/intersection of these four areas helps clarify one's purpose.

The Japanese word combines two elements: *iki*, meaning life, and gai meaning value or purpose. Together, they represent finding joy in the purpose of one's life. However, this concept is very much connected to the role one plays in society or an organization for the greater good. It emphasizes harmony, balance, and the interconnectedness of all things.

From a personal standpoint, ikigai can be a valuable tool in directing one's career path. Take for example Tomoe Gozen (1157-1247), a famous female Japanese Samurai warrior. In a time when women warriors were extremely rare, Tomoe found her ikigai mastering the martial arts along with unwavering loyalty to the Bushido code.

She is renowned as an archer, swords woman, and equestrian along with her bravery in battle, often leading charges against the enemy. Several modern anime and manga characters are representations of her.

Tomoe's story illustrates how ikigai can manifest in breaking societal norms by excelling in one's chosen field regardless of societal pressures.

Another more contemporary modern example would be the female Japanese artist, Yayoi Kusama, best known for her iconic polka dot pumpkins; one red and the other yellow. Like me, she was born and raised on a farm and knew it was not what she wanted for her life!

She began to draw and paint, consumed by it, finding her passion. Her parents, especially her mother, were not pleased; this caused conflict. In fact, Yayoi sent her drawings to Georgia O'Keefe, who was taken by her work, and encouraged her to move to America to meet contemporaries like Andy Warhol. She moved to America and entered the modern art scene in New York. The rest is history.

From an early age, Kusama experienced mental health struggles and hallucinations. Art became her way of expressing her struggles. Facing many challenges and driven by her passion, she has used her unique perspective to challenge perceptions and create art that resonates with viewers. At 95 years old, she is currently the highest-paid female artist in the world, painting and drawing every day. Now that is finding your ikigai!

By discovering your ikigai and aligning your goals and purpose with it, you will find more meaning, peace, and wisdom. There are many people who go through life searching for their meaning, wondering why they are on this Earth. I too know that feeling, and there is hope!

After the accidents of 2005 and 2007, I was in despair and crisis. How would I ever navigate the world with my condition? Because of the accident, I became more focused and found sharing the concepts of the Code of Bushido, Ikigai and Ganbaru to give hope to others was my life's purpose. If life hands you lemons, try making lemonade!

Ikigai can also be an important part of organizational structure. This is demonstrated in the Japanese concept of Kaizen or continual improvement. Used extensively in various Japanese manufacturing companies, it allows for input from anyone within the manufacturing process.

It recognizes that organizations work best when the right person is in the right place with the right idea at the right time resulting in the best solution or product. The right person in the right place goes a long way in insuring teams function at peak performance and goals are attained.

Ganbaru

Unfortunately, the best laid plans can go astray. This is where Ganbaru comes into play. A uniquely Japanese word, it is best translated as determination or perseverance often used for encouragement in demanding situations, it embodies the concept of doing your best and never giving up, regardless of the circumstances.

Remember the 2011 Tohoku Earthquake and Tsunami? The devastation was heartbreaking. Whole towns were destroyed, and the loss of life was staggering. Even today, parts of northeastern Japan remain restricted in the aftermath of the destruction. Despite these circumstances, the determination to rebuild persists as once-devastated areas arise anew.

In the aftermath, people shared resources and encouraged each other by shouting *Ganbatte*—never give up! This word was often heard in the aftermath of the 2011 Tohoku Earthquake and Tsunami to encourage the people of northeast Japan. It speaks to the indomitable human spirit and the desire to keep moving forward, regardless.

Ganbatte, the imperative of Ganbaru, can also be translated as the command "Go for Broke." Interesting that this English translation was the motto of the American 100th/442nd Regimental Combat Team, comprised of Nisei (second generation Japanese American) soldiers during World War II.

Renowned for their courage and toughness, these men exemplified their units' motto, becoming the most highly decorated unit in US Military history for its size and length of time in service. They were without equal.

Their unwavering resolve resonates deeply with me. I remember my dad saying, "Tsugawas never quit;" moving forward was our only option. It is that kind of determination that hastened my recovery from TBI and is needed to succeed in our highly competitive world.

My Mother always said there was a solution regardless of the situation. To me it was like yin and yang; if I had a problem, there were solutions out there. I learned to never quit. Her persuasive way and admonition taught me some day I might even provide someone else's solution.

Conclusion

Code of Bushido, Ikigai and Ganbaru; each of these three concepts by itself is a powerful tool for one's life or organization. Combined they represent your roadmap to success.

My experience with TBI was a transformational point in my life. Like the phoenix, I was able to rise above the ashes and become a TBI survivor. What I learned from this journey fueled a passion to help others overcome life's challenges by implementing these concepts in their lives and organizations.

Life can be a struggle, but it does not have to defeat us. Building on the firm moral principles in the code of Bushido, you can rise above circumstances and follow your passion through Ikigai.

Combined with the determined persistence of Ganbaru, you can overcome life's challenges.

Let me, the Samurai Strategist, be your guide on your epic journey!

Ganbatte!

About Lori Tsugawa

 Lori Tsugawa, a third-generation Japanese American and Samurai descendant, is an inspirational speaker, published author, and life coach. She helps individuals and organizations using the ancient concepts from her Japanese heritage.

Her purpose-driven approach uses the moral foundation of Bushido, the Okinawan concept of Ikigai (finding one's purpose), and the perseverance of Ganbaru. These principles form an unstoppable approach to overcoming challenges and building a strong foundation.

Growing up in a predominantly Caucasian community, Lori did not appreciate her heritage until later in life. After overcoming two serious auto collisions, her resilience informs her guidance for others facing challenges. Lori's book, Let the Samurai Be Your Guide, explores the Bushido Code's relevance today.

Lori holds a BA in Art from Portland State University and is active in various cultural organizations. She is married with two sons, a daughter-in-law, and five grandchildren.

To get Lori's gift, go to: www.LOTbook.net/gift/Lori

Beauty and the Beast

The Transforming Power of Beauty and Love
By Dr. Marta Kassai

Have you thought of fairy tales as parables? On the surface, they are beautiful stories for children about love, beauty, heroes, and happiness. But there is a hidden meaning behind them.

Take, for instance, the tale of *Beauty and the Beast*. The power of true love transforms the ugly Beast into a handsome prince. There is the usual struggle between good and evil, but in the end, good wins.

In these tales, we often read about a kind and pure-hearted princess full of compassion toward others, obedient and selfless, who does not shy away from manual labor and menial tasks. She has a cheerful disposition. Juxtaposed to her is a wicked stepmother, stepsister, or fairy who wants to destroy the innocent girl out of envy, greed, deep hatred, or lust for power. This wicked person is proud, selfish, and won't lift a finger to work.

These fairy or folk tales were passed on by mouth from generation to generation until someone gathered them and published them in books like the Grimm Brothers did in Germany in the early 19th century. These tales reveal the wisdom of the folks. A wisdom that grew out of their life experiences and deep faith. Faith that lasting happiness and society where people flourish results from being good, charitable, honest, industrious, and unselfish. There is a lesson to learn in every fairy tale. Folks knew children learn from these tales about beautiful princesses and handsome heroes that defeat evil.

The evil queen in *Snow White* is filled with envy and rage because Snow White is more beautiful than she is. Her envy grows into an uncontrollable rage that kills the innocent, kind, and lovely Snow White whose beauty surpasses hers. But in the end, good conquers evil. Snow White is resurrected, marries the prince who falls in love with her beauty, and the evil queen dies at their wedding feast.

Evil is powerless over beauty that is matched with an inner beauty of kindness, compassion, generosity, humility, and a joyful attitude. Evil represents the cardinal sins of pride, greed, envy, unjustified anger or raging hatred, gluttony, and sloth. While good represents kindness, charity, humility, diligence, patience, and self-control. The seventh cardinal sin and virtue being lust, and chastity, respectively, is not addressed in children's fairy tales in a sexual content.

Lust is not always sexual. One can lust for power or have an unquenchable desire for wealth and money, or pleasure through narcotics. Chastity is not just abstinence from extramarital sex, or all sex as in celibacy. Chastity also means purity, such as purity of heart. We're told that Snow White had a pure heart.

Someone with a pure heart is sincere and has a genuine desire to do good. It's a person with a clear conscience who seeks the truth and is filled with compassion. "Blessed are the pure of heart for they shall see God." (Matthew 5:8, RSV-CE) is one of the eight beatitudes spoken by Christ. A pure heart is spiritually enlightened and is connected to the divine.

Lust is an intense desire or craving for pleasure. It focuses on self-satisfaction rather than the care and respect of others. It makes no commitment to anyone but self. Lust looks at others as objects for personal gratification. It's dehumanizing.

A lustful person will lose respect not just for others, but also for oneself. Just like the prodigal son who squandered his inheritance on loose women and ended up feeding swine of a farmer in a faraway country just to get by and avoid dying of hunger. To a Jew for whom swine are unclean animals, this must have been the lowest one can sink to. He lost all self-respect.

The son comes to his senses, returns to his father, and begs him to take him back not as his son, but as a hired servant. The father wouldn't hear of it. He accepts him and throws a big celebration that his lost son, who was dead, returned to him alive, who was lost and is found. (Luke 15:11-32, RSV-CE) The son is truly transformed. This parable, told by Jesus, illustrates how much joy our heavenly Father has over one sinner who repents. There is much wisdom in this parable for those who have ears to hear.

Similarly, there is much hidden wisdom in *Snow White and the Seven Dwarfs*. The innocent, pure-hearted young girl runs for her life to hide from her evil stepmother, the queen, who wants to kill her because she is more beautiful. Snow White is dressed in all the virtues little kids should imitate, like kindness, charity, purity of heart, and humility. She diligently keeps the home in order and provides a meal each day. While the queen represents all the vices children should avoid; pride, envy, hatred, rage, greed, sloth, and lust for being the most beautiful in the entire world at all costs.

One of my favorite fairy tales is *Sleeping Beauty*. It's also a struggle between good and evil, like most tales are. Sleeping Beauty is a princess born in a faraway kingdom. The king and the queen throw a big party to celebrate their daughter's birth. They invite everyone except one wicked fairy who gets so angry she curses the infant that on her 16th birthday she will prick her finger on a spindle and die. The invited good fairies try their best to lessen the curse such that instead of dying, the young princess will fall into a deep sleep for one hundred years.

The princess indeed pricks her finger on a spindle on her 16th birthday and immediately falls into a deep sleep. As the years go by, an impenetrable, thorny rose bush grows all around the castle. One day, a young prince who heard about the story cuts through all the thorny bushes, finds Sleeping Beauty, and wakes her up with a kiss. The entire court then wakes up. Sleeping Beauty and the prince get married and live happily ever after.

What is the hidden wisdom in this story? What does the symbolic act of pricking one's finger and falling asleep for a long time represent? It's not as far out as you think. Young, innocent girls are hurt all the time. What kind of hurt would cause them to shut down and surround themselves with an impenetrable wall of thorns? The girl is beautiful, has everything going for her, then a great tragedy happens, and time froze. Everything stops. Darkness sets in, and there is no way to awaken her from this deep coma. Or is there?

Finding true love often brings about healing. Love has a transforming power. But it takes great love to cut through all the thorns. He who tries may be pricked by those thorns over and over. When he finally gets through, reaches the true self, and awakens her so that she, too, can love, the rewards are heavenly.

We are all born innocent and beautiful into a world that is not so innocent and not always beautiful. God gave us free will to choose good or turn away from doing good. To choose good is to choose God because God is all good, the highest good, and infinite good. To turn away from good is to turn away from God.

When the Israelites get to the Promised Land, before they enter, they make a covenant with God before Moses. In this covenant, the Lord tells them: "I have set before you life and death, blessing and curse; therefore choose life that you and your descendants may live." (Deuteronomy 30:19, RSV-CE)

God gave ten commandments to guide his people to choose life. These commandments established a moral and ethical framework for society. They are fundamental to life, for a society to function and prosper. Even today, the laws of our western civilization are based on these commandments. Breaking these commandments leads to death, the death of society.

God is not only all good, but he is life. When Moses asks God what His name is, God reveals his name as "I AM WHO AM"; "Say this to the people of Israel, I AM has sent me to you." (Exodus 3:14, RSV-CE)

René Descartes, the French philosopher, said in 1637, "Cogito, ergo sum" which is Latin for "I think, therefore I am." God is communicating to Moses that He is, that He exists, that He is life itself. Life comes from God, He lives in us, His Spirit lives in us.

When his Spirit leaves us, we die. That's not what we'll find on the death certificate for the cause of death. What's listed is what caused the death of the body. Body is matter. Matter dies. Spirit is not matter. The Spirit does not die. It lives forever. "Do you not know that you are God's temple and that God's Spirit dwells in you?" (1 Corinthian 3:16, RSV-CE)

Hans Driesch (1867-1941), prominent biologist of the early 20th century, claimed that "life is from life" rather than arising spontaneously from non-living matter. No one to date could prove it otherwise. We know that life requires certain basic elements like oxygen, hydrogen, carbon, and nitrogen, the elements that make up proteins. However, no life has ever spontaneously formed from these components in a sealed bottle, even after extended periods of time.

Although these elements of life exist on Mars, we could not find any life in soil samples from Mars. Yet here on Earth in just one cubic centimeter (the size of a dice) there are a staggering number of microorganisms ranging from millions to billions: 10 million to 1 billion bacteria along with various fungi, protozoa, and viruses. No one can argue that there was not enough time for life to evolve on Mars. Mars is about 4.6 billion years old, like the age of Earth. Yet no life has been discovered in spite that the potential for life exists. What is missing is the seed of life.

Cinderella is another astonishingly beautiful young maiden whose mother dies early. Her wicked stepmother and two proud stepsisters are cruel to her. They take away her beautiful clothes, make her do hard work, and mock her. The departing words of her mother were "My dear child, be good and pious, then the good God will always protect you and I will look down on you from heaven and be near you."

Cinderella remained good and pious despite the daily harsh treatments she received from her wicked stepsisters and stepmother. Her big break comes when the king throws a festival for his son. He invites all the beautiful young ladies in the land so his son can choose a bride.

Cinderella is transformed by her fairy godmother into a beautiful princess. She wears the most beautiful dress at the festival. Her stepsisters and stepmother can't recognize her. The prince wants to dance only with her and falls deeply in love.

Cinderella escapes, puts on her shabby gray clothes and wooden slippers, and pretends to be asleep in the kitchen. When her stepmother and sisters return from the festival, they suspect nothing.

The prince sets out to find Cinderella with the glass slipper in hand that fell off Cinderella's foot when she fled the festival. To the horror of Cinderella's stepmother, the shoe fits Cinderella perfectly. The prince is thrilled to have found his true love. They get married and live happily ever after.

It strikes me what a central role beauty plays in fairy and folk tales: *Beauty and the Beast, Snow White and the Seven Dwarfs, Cinderella, and Sleeping Beauty*, just to name a few. What distinguishes the heroines from other beautiful woman in the stories is their inner beauty and virtues that are contrasted with the vices of the other beauties.

It's not just the heroine that is beautiful, her evil opposite, her stepmother, the evil queen, her cruel sisters, and stepsisters are also beautiful. However, the heroine's beauty surpasses all others.

She is not only the most beautiful physically but also spiritually, by being good and kind, pure and humble, and compassionate. While her opponent is endowed with the vices of pride, greed, envy, hatred, and rage. Sometimes, the heroin outwits her opponent and appears intellectually superior, but is mistaken for being stupid by others. Beauty, for instance, is well-read and smart, but her greedy and proud sisters think she is stupid.

Outward beauty is a physical manifestation of the inner beauty of being virtuous; that is compassionate, kind, pure-hearted, industrious, patient, and honest. In addition, having the intellectual advantage of being smart and clever makes the character whole and invincible.

St. Bonaventure, a brilliant 13th-century Franciscan theologian with a doctorate from the University of Paris, where he also served as a professor, wrote extensively about beauty. His great insight was that beauty is not just a superficial attribute but reflects the divine. Beauty is a manifestation of God's goodness and perfection. Observing the beauty of nature gives us a glimpse of God's presence in the world.

There is harmony and a certain orderliness in beauty. It awakens the soul and leads us toward the divine. St. Bonaventure talks about the transformative power of beauty. True beauty will inspire us to be virtuous and good. He encourages us to contemplate the beauty all around to deepen our spiritual journey toward the heart of God. That is love.

I inspire you to look beautiful as a reflection of your inner beauty, not for your sake, but for the sake of others. Think of beauty as an inspiration for others to be good and virtuous.

Be beautiful not to get more from others, but to give more to others. Beauty is a gift. It creates harmony, a pleasant environment where people become more open and relaxed and are inspired to be good. This giving attitude will make you look even more beautiful to others.

When you're not taking care of yourself to look good, it may convey to others that they're not important to you, and you don't care. What kind of relationship does that build? So, always look your most beautiful. Do it for the sake of others, to make them feel good and important.

Think of how you reacted when a handsome, well-dressed person with good mannerism approached you. How did that make you feel? Then place yourself next to someone who looks neglected. Her hair is not combed, and she is wearing some shabby outfit, not because she can't afford decent clothes, but because either she doesn't care or is lazy. How does that make you feel?

My point is to aim to look beautiful because it makes others feel good and appreciated.

About Dr. Marta Kassai

Marta is a religious refugee from communism. During her teenage years, her family fled to the US with the sponsorship of the Mazdaznan movement after their underground faith was discovered and its leader was condemned to imprisonment.

In California, Marta enrolled at Mt. San Antonio Junior College, then transferred to Pomona College for her BA. She pursued receiving her Ph.D. in Chemistry at UC Berkeley under the direction of Nobel Prize winner Melvin Calvin.

Marta began her career at DuPont in Wilmington, DE, in Medical Products. After 12 years, she joined a Bay Area startup as Director of Research. She later held positions as Project and Program Manager at leading biotech and pharmaceutical companies in the San Francisco Bay Area and served as Head of Project Management in Manufacturing at Watson Pharmaceuticals in Southern California.

After leaving the corporate world to care for her mother, Marta started her own business in Cosmetics. As an Independent Beauty Consultant, she advises women on rejuvenating skin care and color cosmetics, helping them look beautiful and gain self-confidence.

To get Marta's gift, go to: www.LOTbook.net/gift/Marta

For the Love of Transformation

Voice for Global Transformation

By Maki Kajiwara

Come rain or shine, singing has been a part of my life. I didn't care when I couldn't get a high score on the college entrance examination. Spending a long time memorizing and practicing my favorite songs was more enjoyable than memorizing essential English vocabulary.

I enjoyed singing songs overnight at the Karaoke studio, returning to the flat only to shower, and then going to work the next day without sleep. It was thrilling being on the stage with my band, although I didn't know how to interact with the audience. With no purpose in life, I would be happy if I could sing.

Until I met two mentors, I struggled with deep emotional pains that originated from the experience with my voice. These affected not only my singing career but also my entire life.

This is the ongoing story of one non-native English speaker from the country of the rising sun who struggled to find who she was and use her voice to change the world.

No Confidence in My Voice

I thought I was born to sing when I was young. Believing I was the best singer in the world, I knew no one could make a better sound than my voice.

I used to practice songs while soaking in the bathtub. One day, my mother said, "I like the voice of your younger sister more than yours because hers sounds softer and better." My mother was my entire world, as my father was abroad for work.

I practiced hard, singing softly to be liked by her. Her response was the same. Gradually I lost my confidence and thought that my voice was not loved- that I was not loved. This made me afraid of singing in front of people because I feared being judged.

But the music gods didn't give up on me. Throughout elementary and junior high school, I was chosen to play piano for hundreds of students singing the school song every Monday. My teachers even let me play the timpani and double bass, which had been purchased for the first time in the school's history.

Although I couldn't pursue advanced training with those instruments because of the lack of a music school in my town, these opportunities made me believe I had a special talent in music.

Karaoke Was My Best Friend

The karaoke bar was the only place I could sing, and one song cost $2. My first experience was at a welcome party for new college students. The senior students picked me to sing a song. I stood up and sang with a powerful sense of fear. When the music ended, everyone applauded me, surprisingly. This unexpected experience made me love Karaoke so much. I got my confidence back little by little.

In my second year, I got a part-time job at the Izakaya (Japanese-style bar) where I requested the owner to let me sing five songs ($10 value) instead of dinner. This bar became my stage. Many guests asked me to sing songs, sometimes together, most times alone. On average, I sang over fifteen songs per night. This made my singing style solid and my voice stronger and clearer.

My Dream Came True

My dream was to join a band to sing songs on stage. At college, I auditioned for student music clubs where many bands were members. I rushed to auditions after my volleyball practice wearing sweaty sports gear with uncombed hair. The student judges laughed at my appearance and told me this club had enough singers, without giving me a chance to sing. I was sad.

One sunny afternoon, I was in my friend's car to go to the patisserie to celebrate completing the examination. One guy was on his bicycle and my friend asked him to join us. He was famous for his band in college. He was going to work at the largest music company. We knew each other but never spoke.

He proposed to go to Karaoke instead of eating sweets. We kept singing for three hours. At night on the same day, my phone rang, and he asked me to join the digital recording of his band next weekend. I didn't need a second to think and said yes. My dream came true suddenly.

Full of Ignorance

The band experience took my voice to the next level. My voice sounded louder, more powerful, and more projected. As I had never taken proper voice training, I frequently failed to hit the right notes. I could not follow the rhythms. Gradually I got frustrated. I verbally attacked the band members and sound engineers when I was told my voice didn't sound right in the recording studio.

Unbelievably, I didn't know the voice I heard myself sounded different from others' ears. I thought the recorder could not capture the full wave of my voice. I complained a lot when I listened to my recorded voice.

That was the moment I could have grown as a musician and a human being if I had been humble enough. I could have understood the science of the voice, trained mine, and gained knowledge of a state-of-the-art music theory and recording environment. It was a sign of my ignorance that I didn't realize it.

I lacked persistence and didn't understand the importance of pursuing my goals or confronting my fear of being judged. What I knew was to move on to the new if I got bored or gave up. So, I quit the band and returned to the Karaoke studio to sing with no obvious goal.

Stuck in The Darkness

I worked at a tech company while continuing to play in the band. The job ensured equal pay and did not require in-person communication. I was fortunate to have exceptional colleagues who were kind enough to buy my CDs and concert tickets. They even shielded me from my boss's anger when a strict client dress code clashed with my blonde hair, which had turned completely blonde after I accidentally fell asleep during a midnight dye session.

Several years after quitting the band, I left this company, moved to the US, and studied at two graduate schools. Luckily, I got a job at a special agency in the United Nations in Switzerland. This was my first exposure to the international environment at work. I was excited that I could serve people globally with my knowledge and experiences in digital technologies.

However, working in English gave me another challenge. The challenge included both a cultural aspect and a technical (pronunciation) one. For example, I grew up in a culture where I didn't need to express myself fully because people read between the lines.

At work, however, I was frequently asked to repeat what I had just said. My words were not understood because I didn't explain fully, and I couldn't pronounce English words properly. This situation was frustrating and my fundamental issues of lack of self-confidence, self-esteem, ignorance, and feeling not loved were coming back day by day.

I didn't leave my job voluntarily; I wanted to continue serving the world despite the challenge of working in English. However, two years after joining the agency, I lost my job because of organizational layoffs. Upon returning to Japan, I felt aimless and worthless. My mental state deteriorated daily, and it felt as though I had entered a tunnel with no way out.

My First Mentor: Her Holiness Sai Maa

One day, my former colleague in Switzerland introduced me to Her Holiness Jagadguru Sai Maa Lakshmi Devi Mishra (Sai Maa). This extraordinary energy master transmutes people energetically. I was interested in spirituality and energy work, so I registered in her program as my last hope.

What she did for me was beyond words. She deeply healed the long-term wounds in my soul and gave me the vitality to live my life again. I burst into tears when she said to me, "You are loved. Believe me. You are loved no matter what. I love you."

During her program, all the dots of my pain were connected instantly. Sai Maa said that there are only two energies: love and fear. Love has a higher frequency that makes you feel open, love, and joy, while fear has a lower frequency that contracts you, like anger, sadness, or resentment.

In my case, I nurtured these fear-based energies (pains or wounds in the soul) and allowed them to control my life. She also said it was not my fault because I could do nothing if I didn't know how to deal with them. Since this program, I have been educating myself. First, I need to be aware of what I feel - love or fear - when I am emotionally triggered. If love, I enjoy it, while I need to purify the energy if it is fear.

I didn't know how to love. The Japanese don't talk or express love openly because of cultural reasons. My parents didn't know how to express their love, though I know they love me. I sang again to love myself as much as I could. I believed in the power of voice even before meeting my second mentor.

My Second Mentor: Roger Love

While searching for a program to become a voice coach and heal people through voice, a friend informed me that the renowned voice coach Roger Love was about to launch the first voice coaching program focused on speaking. I followed my intuition and eagerly joined the program.

Once the program started, I realized I knew nothing about the voice. I knew diaphragmatic breathing but had never learned why it's important for speaking. I didn't know the voice was the instrument to showcase the emotion of both speaking and singing. And the method that helped me change the most was Speak Like Singing.

I got his official coaching qualification, but I still have a lot of work to do. Roger spent an hour correcting my pronunciation of two letters, "R" and "L." He told me to open my mouth vertically instead of horizontally to pronounce "L." I failed many times, but finally, I made it.

193

I felt guilty for using him as my English teacher, but thanks to his dedication and persistence, I broke down the barriers of my fear and shame by using my voice. I learned that it's not embarrassing to show my weaknesses to others. This was a new awareness of the power of voice for transformation.

The more I studied his methods, the more confirmation I received. These methods work perfectly for non-native English speakers who love singing. People love singing because singing makes them feel alive, free, authentic, and good.

Using a singing approach can set the bar lower to highlight their personality in speaking English. I had no confidence when I spoke English before. After applying this Speak Like Singing method, I can showcase my personality in any language just as well as I can in Japanese.

Voice for Global Transformation

Culturally, Japanese people speak monotone because they consider it polite. I found the same in international organizations as well. The representatives from governments or research institutions are so focused on delivering their points quickly that they can't pay attention to their voices and audiences.

I recall several impressive speeches. The speakers weren't native English speakers; however, they made us laugh hard and delivered the key messages succinctly. Their speeches mixed the speed faster and slower with melodies, pauses, and hand gestures. The most important ingredient that made their speeches impressive was that they highlighted their personalities and emotions in their voice. These impressive speeches remained in our memories and often led the discussion on global issues.

These memories confirmed that the path I had taken was the right one. Accents, pronunciation, and grammar are not important for moving people emotionally and transforming the world. Rather, highlighting yourself authentically with your voice is critical. Mistakes and failures are learning. Challenges are chances to grow. To be authentic, love and self-acceptance are the key. These are what I learned from my lifelong journey of studying spirituality and singing.

I am still in the process of transformation and have much to learn. I am imperfect, but this is my current form of perfection. If we can embrace and express who we are now, our voices can contribute to global transformation.

If we can embrace and express who we are now, our voices can contribute to global transformation.

About Maki Kajiwara

 Maki Kajiwara is a Japanese international civil servant dedicated to improving access to medicine, quality care, and health service delivery with digital technologies for nearly 200 countries. With a background in global health and ICTs, Maki bridges the gap between health services and technology, ensuring inclusive, effective, and user-friendly digital solutions. Since 2023, she has been advancing digitalization in traditional Medicine in India.

Born into a modest family, Maki received a rich musical education, playing various instruments. She discovered the liberating power of her voice, which had been a life-saving force for her. Besides her professional work, Maki serves as a voice coach for non-native English speakers, helping them improve and transform their voices.

Maki holds master's degrees from the Johns Hopkins Bloomberg School of Public Health and Syracuse University School of Information Studies, and a bachelor's degree from the University of Tsukuba.

To get Maki's gift, go to: www.LOTbook.net/gift/Maki

For the Love of Transformation

Dream Big, Play Small, and Live Fully
By Timothy Aleong

Life Happens to Me

It was a beautiful sunny day on September 11, 2001, in New York City. The previous day, I had been in Madison for a friend's wedding and had arrived back late to my corporate apartment in Battery Park. As a result, that morning I was running late for a meeting at my client's office near Penn Station.

I stood across the street from the subway entrance that was near the South Tower. A loud explosion echoed through the air as the first plane struck the North Tower. My initial thought was that it was a bomb, recalling the 1993 World Trade Center bombing and the urgent need to get far away.

In what felt like the longest seconds of my life, time seemed to slow as debris fell to the ground. Amidst the chaos and the sounds of screams, I saw people struck by the falling wreckage, lying motionless on the ground.

Realizing I had only moments to find cover before the storm of debris intensified, I stood exposed in the middle of the street with no protection. I instinctively raised my small briefcase over my head, hoping it would shield me. However, it would not have stopped something as heavy as a plane's tire falling from over a hundred stories above, as I would soon learn.

Searching for refuge, I feared I could not reach safety in time. I noticed a driver abandoning the cab of his box truck and diving under its side. Following him, I slid under the side of the truck and immediately after, debris rained down on the truck and street. I was lucky to be alive.

For the rest of the day, I witnessed horrific events unfold. When the South Tower collapsed, I was engulfed in the thick dust cloud with many others.

I felt helpless, scared, and numb. For many years after that day, I stopped dreaming and didn't fully live my life. I often questioned why I had survived such a horrific event when so many others had not. For years, I drifted through life without proper direction or goals. Subconsciously, I decided not to dream anymore, letting life lead me rather than taking control. Anxiety became a constant companion, undermining my ability to manage my emotions.

In 2018, I made a conscious decision to reclaim my life and focus on genuinely enjoying it. While my life is far from perfect—and perfection is not the goal—being human means that each day offers an opportunity to work towards the life I envision.

We dedicate ourselves to our jobs and education, so why shouldn't we also strive for the life we desire? As I wrote this chapter, I grappled with why I was not living fully after my close brush with death. My heightened fear of dying had transformed into a fear of living and being seen. This fear fueled my anxiety and a desperate need for control. My perspective on life and for many years after, was that life happened to me.

Dream Big

Dreaming big is crucial for personal growth and forward momentum in life. It is not achieving the dream that brings happiness, but the journey of progress and growth in pursuit of it. Life is constantly changing; every second of every day brings us closer to the future, and we can't stop this change. Since change is inevitable, setting goals to achieve our dreams is essential.

For many, dreaming big is challenging because we doubt our dreams can come true. As we envision what is possible, our inner critic often questions our aspirations, saying things like, "You are not good enough." This inner critic can be harsh, but dreaming big requires us to question and challenge our beliefs. A belief is a thought that through experiences and emotions, we hold as true, shaped by our past and current environments. While it is unnecessary to discard all our beliefs, it is important to challenge those that do not serve us.

When we miss out on a promotion or cannot land a job, we might be tempted to believe that we simply are not good enough, that such successes are reserved for others. An alternate viewpoint, we might recognize it as a skills gap, something that can be bridged with the right training and effort. If you frequently are overly self-critical, it may reflect your underlying beliefs.

Our brains, specifically the Reticular Activating System (RAS), filter information based on what we are focused on. If you have a limiting belief, like "My dreams can't come true," your RAS will highlight evidence supporting that belief. But by challenging these beliefs, asking questions, and being curious, especially about limiting ones, you can find evidence to the contrary.

Reflect on your own limiting beliefs. Do you think, "I'll never find the one," "I'll never be successful," or "I'm not good enough"? Take a moment to consider these thoughts and write about them. A powerful way to recognize how these beliefs might be holding you back is to consider goals that seemed impossible to your younger self five or ten years ago, but that you have since achieved. Setting ambitious goals to pursue your dreams is a vital step in challenging these limiting beliefs and fostering personal growth.

Play Small

In the previous section, we explored the importance of dreaming big and being curious about your beliefs. However, the enormity of these dreams and goals can be overwhelming. It's at this point that the inner critic often resurfaces, reinforcing limiting beliefs with thoughts like, "Why bother? That dream is unattainable," creating a cycle of doubt and hesitation.

Our minds are inherently complex, often defaulting to avoid discomfort from new experiences that challenge us. Yet, it's through these very experiences that we can discover profound joy and fulfillment. In project management, a critical aspect is breaking down a project's goal into individual tasks that are then grouped and organized.

For instance, if you aim to build your first bookshelf, you start by planning each step: deciding on the size, type, materials, tools, and finish. Though building a bookshelf could be completed in a day with no distractions, most goals however require more time and consistent effort, especially when juggling daily life responsibilities.

Often, we approach big dreams intending to complete them in one go. When this isn't workable, the dream, like an unfinished bookshelf, sits abandoned in the basement, waiting for a perfect moment that rarely comes.

The key to progress lies in committing to two or three small tasks each day that move you toward your goal, no matter how minor they may seem. If you have a habit of not finishing what you set out to do, it's crucial to be kind to yourself. The issue is not with you; it's about you not yet having the skills or tools to accomplish the goal. With the right approach, you can achieve it.

Start by breaking down your big dreams into small, actionable steps. For example, when I trained for my first marathon, despite not being a runner or enjoying running, I committed to a daily training plan. The plan started modestly: a 0.5-mile walk on the first day, gradually increasing the distance each day thereafter. This incremental approach built my confidence in the progress I made each day. Eight months later, I completed my first marathon.

Similarly, we shouldn't expect to achieve our dreams without gradual, consistent effort. Consistency is key. Working towards your goals, in small daily increments, aligns with the ongoing demands of life. For instance, if your goal is to learn Italian, apps today offer small daily exercises. Learning one word a day may seem insignificant, but over a year, it accumulates into a substantial vocabulary.

The main idea is to break down your big dream into smaller actionable items until they can't be simplified further. These minor tasks build upon one another, gradually increasing your confidence and momentum. To maintain this momentum, it's helpful to tackle these tasks early in the day when energy levels and focus are typically higher. Consistently ask yourself, "What are the smallest two to three things I can do today to make progress?" This way, you keep your dream at the forefront and ensure steady, incremental progress despite life's inevitable distractions.

Live Fully

A fulfilling life isn't about achieving your dreams; it's about the journey of pursuing them. Often, we find that once we've attained what we thought we wanted, the reality doesn't quite match our expectations. Humans are naturally inclined to feel happier when they are growing and stretching themselves, yet we also have an inner critic designed to keep us safe from discomfort, whether physical or mental. This creates a paradox: the very discomfort that can lead to growth and fulfillment is also what our minds often try to avoid.

Through my exploration of various practices and concepts, I have learned that there is no one-size-fits-all solution. However, several techniques have consistently helped me. I will share three techniques. These are not magic pills, but practices that require daily commitment. Everyone is unique, so it's important to find what works for you and discard what does not.

One technique that has had a profound impact on me is journaling. Putting thoughts into physical words on a page can bring clarity to the swirling ideas in your mind. Writing can tap into your unconscious mind, much like an iceberg where most of its mass lies hidden below the surface.

By externalizing your thoughts, you can better examine the self-talk that often goes unnoticed. This exercise can reveal that the things you say to yourself are things you would never say to a dear friend. I begin my journaling practice by listing three things I am grateful for. This trains my mind to focus on the positives in life, directing my RAS to notice and appreciate positive experiences.

Meditation is another technique that has helped me become more of an observer in life. Initially, meditation can be challenging because it involves doing something new and potentially uncomfortable, which may trigger the inner critic. However, with consistent effort and by starting small—with just one to five minutes—you can build this habit. Even on busy days, a short meditation session can noticeably improve your day. Finding time for these practices might seem daunting, but it's about deliberate, daily practice rather than quantity.

Physical exercise is the third technique, and it's crucial not just for physical health but for mental well-being. While many people associate exercise with weight loss and physical fitness, it also triggers the release of chemicals in the body that contribute to positive mental states. These include endorphins (natural painkillers and mood elevators), serotonin (stabilizes mood and reduces depression and anxiety), norepinephrine (improves attention and motivation), and others.

Regular movement helps generate these chemicals, making it easier to tackle daily tasks and maintain a positive outlook. For example, I have found that after exercising, whether it's walking or playing a sport, I feel more energized and motivated to complete even mundane chores.

On the flip side, daily stress can cause an imbalance of chemicals, but exercise and other positive practices can counteract this effect. The key to a fulfilling life lies not in the destination but in the daily work that helps us grow, overcome challenges, and maintain a positive mindset.

Life Happens for Me

Reflecting on 9/11, I have now come to embrace the notion that life happens for me, steering me towards a greater purpose. There is a profound reason I was spared, a reason I continue to live and breathe. Perhaps it is to share my story, to inspire resilience and hope in others.

Dreaming big and taking control of your life's direction is essential. Without clear goals, life can easily go adrift, leaving you feeling unfulfilled and unexcited about where you have ended up. Your inner critic may try to keep you in your comfort zone, but it's crucial to stay curious and question your assumptions. Just as each person may interpret the exact painting differently, your current beliefs shape how you see the world. By exploring other perspectives, you open yourself to new possibilities.

Once you have set your dreams, break them down into the smallest possible steps. If you are unsure of all the steps, seek guidance from someone who has already achieved a similar dream. Learn from their journey and start by taking just two to three small actions each day. Consistency and accountability are key; as you complete these tasks, no matter how minor, your confidence will grow. This might be as simple as making a phone call or writing a single line in a business plan for that day.

While pursuing your dreams, don't forget to enjoy life. Journaling can help you manage your inner dialog and focus on the positive aspects of your life. Begin each day by noting three things you are grateful for, creating a positive mindset that can influence your entire day. Use your journal to track progress on your daily tasks, reinforcing your commitment to your goals. Meditation, even for a few minutes, can be a transformative practice, helping you stay centered and focused. Physical activity can boost your mood and motivation, thanks to the natural chemicals it releases in your body.

So, dream big, play small, and live fully!

About Timothy Aleong

 Timothy Aleong is a dedicated student of life, committed to sharing the knowledge and experiences that have shaped his personal journey.

With a diverse educational background, Timothy holds a Bachelor of Engineering from McGill University, an MBA from Boston College, a degree in Computational Finance from the University of Washington and professional certifications in Finance and Project Management.

Timothy has cultivated a strong foundation in technical disciplines, equipping him with a unique perspective on complex problem-solving and decision-making processes. His passion for learning extends beyond formal settings, as he actively seeks opportunities to engage with everyday individuals, sharing insights, and strategies that have proven effective in his own life.

Timothy's approach is grounded in the belief that knowledge should be accessible to all. As Timothy continues to explore new horizons in his life, he remains committed to helping others navigate their challenges and celebrate their successes. His journey reflects the importance of continuous learning and the value of sharing one's experiences to uplift and inspire others.

To get Timothy's gift: www.LOTbook.net/gift/Timothy

A Tale of Transformation

By Caroline Stamu-O'Brien

"Nothing endures but change."
-Heraclitus

I often dream of my long-lost childhood. It brings back beautiful memories of how it was. The sea waves kiss the golden sand. Radiant sun tans my skin like an ancient trophy. An exotic one. I could tell you stories about sunburn.

Salty water and wind whispers breeze away the heat. The strawberry ice cream dripping off the cone. Hiding away under a parasol. Playing beach volleyball or badminton.

I remember being mesmerized by petunias' spiritual purity. Marigolds and roses infuse my soul with their scents. The acacia trees with their fern-like look, the grace of the weeping willow, the heart-shaped leaves of the poplar tree, the tamarisk, and silk trees along roadsides, all enrich my experience.

But all this beauty in my adolescence was engulfed by a black hole: the loss of my father. As Jethro Tull describes it...

> *"And he was too old to rock and roll*
> *And he was too young to die."*

My personal transformation started during my early childhood. It happened in the company of my father. I fondly remember minute details blurred by passing time. They come and go, keeping me in touch with my ancestry. The hope of full recollection that I was once fifteen years old brings tears

211

into my eyes. He enjoyed calling me *"dad's American girl"* and *"my little doctor"* even though he never studied English, but he picked it up fast.

Did you know that the *Voice of America (VOA)* facilitated my connection with the Western world via shortwave radio? It happened before the fall of the *Iron Curtain*. It is all in the *VOA*'s archives: the latest scientific discoveries in science and medicine, the domestic and international states of affairs. I remember everyone was talking about the first successful human heart transplant by Christiaan Barnard in 1967. I was mesmerized and hooked, dreaming about a utopian world, so far away and out of my reach, impossible to touch. But somehow, I had an inner knowing that it was possible.

I used to look forward to my clandestine midnight entertainment listening to the broadcast intro with the lyrics and tunes of *"The Yankee Doodle."*

> *"Yankee Doodle went to town*
> *A-riding on a pony*
> *Stuck a feather in his hat*
> *And called it macaroni."*
> *(CHORUS) Yankee Doodle keep it up, Yankee Doodle dandy!*
> *Mind the music and the step, and with the girls be handy!*

In an improvised duo, dad and I hummed the tune.

What Does History Have to do with it?

Since the day I started reading *"The Death of a President"* by William Manchester, I became very drawn to American history. The "why" and the "how" kept my interest at peak, despite my limited understanding. I was just opening my eyes to how the world worked and the strange facts. Periodically, father reminded me of the inspiration for my first name, President Kennedy's daughter, which gave me a deep sense of connection.

Names rich in history made me feel exiled since birth to a country which I did not choose. Then, halfway through the savoring of this historical masterpiece, my father met the sudden death of JFK. In that moment, he became my President. We are all influenced by our early upbringing and experiences. It was then that my younger self kneeled at his grave with the promise to become what he had instilled in me.

Unbeknownst to me, my fascination with America became a reality eleven years later. The unique transcendental feeling of walking the ground and planting my roots is intertwined with a prominent history and a grand sense of adherence.

I have been moving through time and history since then, a sophisticated and beautiful journey which has left indelible marks on my soul. History would not exist without the concept of time and strong leaders. It took President Regan to *"Tear down this wall,"* a reverberating slogan against communism. I grew up with stories about the ancient Macedonian Empire and its plunge into civil war that led to people with no country. Just like others have witnessed the rise of Rome in Caesar's time and its later demise, so have I witnessed drastic socio-political changes, civil unrest, uprising, street confrontations, and a revolution. This alone was enough to compel me to choose my country. A privilege, indeed!

The Magic of Art

My adolescence was shaped by various genres of weekly Top Ten music hits.

"Don't, don't you want me?
You know I can't believe it when I hear that you won't see
me..."

These lyrics are the seal of perfection by *The Human League*, revealing the meaning of deep connections.

This musical refuge from the quotidian life spanned through my early twenties. Between the *VOA* and *Radio Free Europe/Radio Liberty*, the two broadcasts maintained a balanced voice in reporting about the events in December 1989. Moments of psychedelic-like euphoria descended upon me from the album *"The Wall."* I was in the "company" of *Pink Floyd* for one week and felt that there was no everlasting youth and eternal life, there was only social isolation. It was time for the demise of communism and the dictatorial regime and the introduction of democracy. I felt a strong connection to the delusions and paintings of van Gogh, the result of mediocrity in the world. There was no *Starry Night* for me!

I remember the long years of medical school, the intense and meticulous study of *Testut's Treatise* and *Gray's Anatomy.* I could not afford to miss a footnote, because the Anatomy exam was the most difficult to pass. Despite exciting experiences during a time of extreme social restrictions and lack of liberty to explore the world, I felt both repressed and oppressed. I started contemplating a new life on a different shore. I did not know that my life would take me to where I belonged.

Everything is energy. You and I are just an exchange of energy. Anything we manifest results from it, whether it is physical or emotional. Just like in the *Heisenberg Uncertainty Principle*, we can never be sure simultaneously of the position and velocity of an electron. As I am the result of both particles and waves, my existence is only probability.

In this ocean of probability, strange circumstances beyond my control threw me on different paths. The twists and turns made me understand the complexity of human life. When I was contemplating my career, I became more aware of the impact of psychological factors on diseases. I came across patients with advanced malignancies with no hope of staying alive, fighting their last battle. Complementary Medicine was in its infancy. This was my defining moment for embracing psychiatry as a field. People wanted to live. It was the power of their mind that kept them going.

Keep the Mind Still

Any little girl holds the key to dominate opportunities. This dominion is called Life, and its transformation starts with deep reflection that this is a necessary journey towards self-discovery. Not everything is inner strength when various degrees of emotions can alter serenity. The main secret is to maintain balance and harmony, and to find equilibrium between personal desires and responsibilities. To touch hearts means to flourish, even when the terrain is rough.

Emotional energy is the most complex that we humans experience. It has both easiness and difficulty to tap into. My past, present, and future have merged as an echo of inner knowing, talent, and interpersonal relationships. My eyes reflect the silence of a shadow, the spontaneous laughter, the joy of feeling at peace, the grievance of loss, the fear of war, the anger about injustice, the unwanted distress, and emptiness as void. Rejection is a catalyst for transformation. My sensibility satisfied those who were selfish, competitive, and devoid of scruples.

The path of mystery paved with clues of multi-dimensions since before Creation is my quest!

Fate whispers the way I perceive things, the way I experience love, the most transformative force. People played key roles in my life as catalysts for major internal and external changes. Yet, the power of man is subjective. Beyond assumptions, through their actions, whether subtle or bold, I achieved revelations.

A feline reminds me of intuition. It is my gift to avoid unforeseen traps, teaching me adaptability. A sense of familiarity with inspiration defines each chapter of my life.

The steppingstone to the new me is coordinated with the universe, engulfed in winds of change. Just like walking through a door, I entered a parallel world, a deeper understanding of human connections where healing and hope are supernova outshining galaxies. I embrace this transformation.

There is beauty in thoughts and ideas, changing the concept of human existence. Take this haiku-poem, for example!

*"The bright moon
lifts from the mountains' shadow
and stands alone in the sky."*
-Li Bai

An ode to Nature and its hidden symmetries, this poem means that the world finds its beauty in symmetry. Seize the window of treasured dreams in 4-D, gate to your uniqueness! Dare to venture into the unknown!

Coincidental as it may seem, challenges I thought were insurmountable were conquered through confidence and fortitude. In despair, persistence was my companion, together with initiated adaptation and a superhuman ability to transmute passions into realizations through emotional alchemy. It is perhaps the desire for originality that is to blame! In all these mature experiences, I cherished clarity.

In short, I embarked on a complex quest for inner and outer transformation, in which harmony is the essence of inner peace.

Only if I could walk through walls. Just imagine for a moment how it would be to pass right through doors! I found that while Euclidean geometry defined my outer transformation, the inner transformation is rich and diverse through the multitude of non-local emotions, feelings, thoughts, and intuition. The distance between defeat and triumph is Riemannian! This inner alignment results from light warping of the geometry of higher dimensional space.

Give Yourself a Voice!

"When I let go of what I am, I become what I might be."
-Lao Tzu

Our sun is an ordinary star, meaningful to our existence; yet our existence would not be exalted without language. Since the dawn of humanity, humans have acquired knowledge used in both oral and written communication. Chomsky stated that effective language skills are paramount during early developmental stages. Not a single child has the option to express a preference. Neither did I. Geographical and cultural circumstances usually impose it.

I remember my first years of studying English in elementary school. During the class, we all had an English first name. I was called Lucy when I preferred Alice, but I embraced Lucy so much more when I became familiar with the sitcom *"I Love Lucy."* Years later, I dreamed of becoming an English teacher, a magnificent journey which pushed me to excel in local and national contests.

The English Language, through its sophistication and economic sense of expression, is representing perfection. While it is difficult to express emotion in written communication, writing enables a level of expression that is difficult to manifest verbally. I find writing to be a venue for expressing suppressed emotions in transformative subjective experiences. Oral expression has its foundation through speech, a wonderful sound device, but it takes one's voice to manifest purpose. To have a voice is so much more: it is the deep manifestation of your soul.

Location in Space

I wake up on a warm summer morning. The nearby park is an oasis of beauty amongst the tall gray city buildings. Only some of them are painted in red brick or blue. There is nothing better than taking a stroll to the farmers' market. My eyes catch a banner of the *"Bread Alone"* stand. A line by Miguel de Cervantes soothes my soul: *"All sorrows are less with bread."* There is so much truth to it.

A lot has changed in this area in the past decades. People pass by enjoying their coffee or making a good market deal. Most apple varieties are $3.00 lb. while Honey Crisp is $4.00 lb. I like any apples. Two vendors are busy with their clients. *"We are cash and Venmo,"* the woman said. I smile and move on.

My ears pick an indistinguishable chatter, like bees pollinating flowers. They keep fading away while I tell myself: there is so much greatness of spirit in the farmer's market. A musician plays Mbira, engulfing the casual street noise in high-pitched rhythmic notes. Life happens all around me in so many ways. I am happy to be part of this vibrant life. Nothing would make me happier than to take a walk with my father. Incidentally, on the fated morning of June 20, 2023, I almost had, but he knew my mission had not been completed yet.

I would like to take my younger self to the dunes of the Atlantic Ocean, to the incandescent sand and salty breeze in a splash of shore-breaking waves. New York both surprises and inspires me. Despite its constant change, it runs deeply through my veins.

About Caroline Stamu-O'Brien, M.D.

Caroline Stamu-O'Brien, M.D. is an established ABPN diplomate physician with extensive experience in psychiatry built upon firm doctoral and post-doctoral training at the Mount Sinai Medical Center in New York City, where she specialized in schizophrenia research and psychopharmacology.

Caroline demonstrated a successful history as an academic and corporate hospital physician. As a medical entrepreneur, she is the Founder of *Integrative Psychiatry of NY* and specializes in clinical psychopharmacology based on an innovative and integrative approach to mental illness. She is continually active in research covering biological and clinical psychiatric aspects of medicine, specifically psychoneurodermatology, psychosis, and apoptosis in schizophrenia.

She is the indie coauthor of *Functional Architecture of the Human Mental*. This monograph provides a new understanding of the human mind from an exacting psychophysics vantage.

Much of her research is published in educationally relevant journals such as Biological Psychiatry, 1999, Journal of the American Academy of Dermatology, 2017, Journal of Clinics in Dermatology, 2023, and Dermatological Reviews, 2023.

To get Caroline's gift: www.LOTbook.net/gift/Caroline

For the Love of Transformation

When Knowing Why Isn't Enough

By Adrienna Harris

As I write this paragraph, tears are running down my face. It is part of a painful story that I thought I would never share with anyone. But I want to assist someone out there who might be in a similar situation. To tell them that no matter what happens, they should never give up on themselves.

On the first night in my new apartment, I sat on the floor trying to figure out how I had ended up there and how I would pay my bills while attending school full-time. With no sofa or love seat in the living room, I felt sad and alone, especially since less than twenty-four hours earlier, I had been living with others.

It feels like just yesterday—I had just returned from running errands when someone met me at the front door before I could even go back inside.

She walked me to my car and told me we would look at some apartments right now. It was the most subtle way of putting someone out without telling them. I felt like someone else wanted me out of the house, and she was orchestrating everything. She guided me through every step of the process, and I felt like I had an out-of-body experience.

I was looking for her to give me some guidance because I didn't know why I was there. Whenever the apartment manager asked a question, I didn't know how to respond. When he asked do you want a one-bedroom, my response was "I guess so." After our apartment viewing, he asked if I wanted to apply. She said yes.

I was taken aback by the demand to get my own place, since I was only working a part time job. It felt like a sudden leap into adulthood, as if I had to paddle fiercely just to keep afloat.

I brought along my bed and highboy dresser. I stumbled upon a yard sale where I snagged a dining room table and two chairs for just $25. Someone gave me a sewing machine stand to use as a TV stand, and some secondhand pots and pans.

Before long, I discovered I was pregnant with my daughter, yet I still hadn't completed my four-year degree. Despite attending several colleges, I couldn't seem to muster the will to finish.

If you have a strong enough reason for doing something, the "how" becomes less of a problem. Have you ever encountered a situation where your reason for pursuing a goal didn't provide the motivation you needed to reach it?

In such cases, the key is to simply start. As you make progress, you'll find unexpected benefits like increased movement, motivation, and momentum—much like the momentum that comes from a compelling "why."

Willingness is defined in Webster's dictionary as relating to the will or power of choosing. Willingness can prevent you from reaching your goals. Just as you decide to take the steps to achieve your goals, you also decide not to start or complete them. Regardless of which decision you make, it is a choice you must make consciously or unconsciously.

Ask yourself these questions: Can I afford to miss the benefits of achieving this goal? What will be the short-term and long-term consequences? Will I regret this decision later in my life?

Are any of these reasons affecting your willingness: too much stress, undefined goals, lack of motivation, fear of failure, low self-esteem, lack of confidence, experiences, accepting the status quo, low energy, health issues, lack of focus, or misconceptions?

If you fully understand the benefits and still choose not to act, you may need to do some soul-searching. **Remember, you can't achieve your goals without finishing. It's important to uncover what's holding you back**. It could be a deeper issue that requires additional resources, support, or professional counseling. This will help you move forward and create consistent commitment.

<u>Commitment and Consistency</u> - After my daughter turned one, I applied to the local college. I bought a notebook and listed all seven days of the week to track my study time. Before classes started, I committed to dedicating the minimum time needed to establish a new habit.

I committed to studying for thirty minutes, three times a week, for my classes. Although this amount was far less than needed to see significant results, it helped me get started and stay consistent. Often, I ended up studying for longer than thirty minutes. I set low expectations intentionally to ensure I could start and maintain the habit.

Plus, this was something I hadn't done consistently for a while and would be crucial for the next three years to complete college. If I couldn't fit in a full 30-minute study session, I made sure to at least complete my homework.

This approach allowed me to achieve my daily study goals, providing early wins to celebrate. These small successes helped me build momentum while establishing a new habit and maintaining consistency.

When the "why" isn't enough, commit to focusing on consistency, as it will yield significant results. Consistency is crucial throughout the entire process, from start to finish, no matter what the goals. **The more consistent, the better the results you'll see.** At the outset, consistency should be your primary focus, as it builds momentum for the rest of the process.

Change Your Mindset - You have heard the saying, "Where the mind goes, the man follows." Thoughts have a tremendous impact on life and accomplishments. By analyzing your thoughts before and after both your failures and successes, you'll likely notice a significant shift in your mindset. You might even realize you had mentally given up before you truly started, or before any failure occurred.

It would be wonderful if you always had a support system of people who could uplift you with their words. However, since this is not the case for most, you need to be patient and understanding with yourself as you gradually shift your mindset towards optimism while working on your goals.

This process will significantly influence your perception of life, your attitude, and your ability to be more positive. Remember, changing your mindset is a journey that takes time, and people will notice the difference in what you say, what you do, how you behave, how you treat yourself and others, and how you show up.

How to Use Your Mindset to Boost Motivation and Achieve Your Goals: Start by telling yourself, "I can do this," "I've got this," "I will cross the finish line," and "I can't wait to see how great this will turn out." Anticipate the thrill of success and recall when you successfully completed other goals.

When opposing thoughts arise, counter them immediately with something authentic, uplifting, and positive. Remember, everything you are working on for growth and development will have its difficulties, pros, and cons.

Limit how much you will talk and think about the negative aspects of the process and your failures along the way. Instead, think about how much better you will be and what you will gain after accomplishing your goals.

Reevaluate The Why - How does the why help fulfill your purpose in life? I considered dropping out of college, but I couldn't because my "why" had become a powerful reason that moved me deeply. I wanted a better life for my daughter and to break the cycle of living in the projects, as my family had.

My situation improved when my "why" became bigger than myself and was tied to my purpose. When your "why" is intricately connected to your life's purpose, it becomes much easier to stay motivated and achieve your goals.

As Viktor E. Frankl wisely noted, those with a "why" to live can endure almost any "how." Each of us has a unique purpose in life. It's crucial to evaluate regularly and potentially revise this purpose, as it may shift.

You may not have considered your life's purpose for many years. I encourage you to take a few moments to reflect and write about your life's purpose, and how it aligns with your current goals.

Connect Your Goals to Your Overall Growth and Development: If your goals don't align with your life purpose, consider how they fit into your short-term and long-term growth. Both work-related and personal goals can boost motivation by showing how they contribute to your overall development.

Review The Benefits - What will the results be besides the fact that it will be completed? Do you know how much it will affect your life? It's crucial to research and write all the benefits for each goal you try to accomplish. Some people are more driven when they fully understand all the benefits of completing their goals.

As a first-generation college graduate, I was intensely focused on my new "why," but I overlooked many of the benefits that came with it. If someone had explained to me the advantages of earning degrees in Management Information Systems and Accounting, I would have been more motivated and could have completed my studies much sooner.

Completing my education opened doors I hadn't imagined. I chose from three job offers, an upgrade from a Nissan Sentra with no air conditioning and an oil leak to a brand-new Honda Accord and move from a one-bedroom apartment with brown panel walls, multicolored carpet with baseboard heating and an air unit in the front room to a two-bedroom apartment that looked like it belonged in a magazine. I gained a retirement plan, took on leadership roles as president of two college clubs, built lasting relationships with fellow students, and secured an internship that provided valuable experience in SQL and Access, enhancing my career prospects.

The benefits went far beyond just accomplishing the goal. Completing my education boosted my confidence, provided a deep sense of fulfillment, and enhanced my resilience. It improved my skills and knowledge, opened new opportunities, and transformed how I viewed my achievements and myself. Identifying and reflecting on both the material and non-material gains from reaching my goals has fueled my motivation and commitment.

Deal With Failure - Failure is a part of life when pursuing goals or personal growth. It's challenging to handle because it demands emotional resilience, practical reflection, and a constructive action plan. How we respond to failure—whether we get back up, try again, and ultimately succeed—depends on our approach to it. For many, failure can have a profound impact, affecting them physically, emotionally, and mentally, and it can be particularly devastating for those who have never experienced it.

As I was trying to finish my education, I attended several universities and changed my major three times. It seemed like no matter what I tried, it didn't work, and I felt like I kept failing repeatedly. It had gotten to where it was affecting me mentally, and I became depressed. I felt like I was a failure, and the only thing that kept me going was my willingness and my why.

How I Dealt with Failure: During this time in my life, I turned to a poem titled "Don't Quit" by Edgar Guest. The poem helped me understand that success is often just failure turned inside out. It resonated deeply with me, as I was going through many of the struggles described in it. I reviewed the poem frequently and kept a copy in the zipper pocket of my purse. Despite becoming very wrinkled, I held on to the original copy and never replaced it.

I made a list of potential obstacles to graduating and noted ways to prevent each one. For instance, since my car was leaking oil and I had only liability insurance, I limited my trips, drove carefully, and checked the oil weekly to avoid problems that could prevent me from attending classes.

It's a harsh reality that some people close to you may wish for your failure rather than your success. During the month I was sick at the start of my pregnancy and the six weeks following my daughter's birth, NO ONE offered financial support—whether for bills, groceries, books, or tuition. Throughout the final three years of college, I worked 20-30 hours a week with minimal resources and no financial assistance from anyone. This raises the bigger question: why didn't they offer help when they saw me struggling?

To this day, I still don't know how I made it. While I was out of work after I had my daughter, I got an eviction notice. I will always be thankful for the nonprofit organization who paid my rent for that month.

Seek Advice Sooner Than Later - Prior to working on any goals, get advice from experts or people who have already accomplished what you are trying to do. You are never on the journey by yourself. Reach out and talk to people and ask for advice. Some things that I experienced would have been avoided if I had asked for advice.

Picture my lunch with a friend from Kimberly Projects, who was curious about my journey as a working parent and college student. She asked how I graduated while raising my daughter, taking 21 credit hours in my final three semesters, and working as an intern. My answer was straightforward: I got started, stayed laser-focused, planned for setbacks, and adjusted my motivation. The rest, as they say, is history.

After graduation, I was honored as the Most Outstanding Management Information Systems Senior. Out of five job interviews, I received three offers: IT Specialist, Systems Business Analyst, and Information Systems Auditor. My new employer, IBM, even provided a $4,000 bonus to assist with my move to a new city. One employer was so impressed with my interview that he increased his offer three times, adding $8,000 each time, acknowledging that no one else had interviewed as well as I did.

On that first night in my new living room, I stood there, reflecting on my journey, and thanking myself for not giving up. It was a moment of profound empowerment, knowing that I had achieved everything on my own terms through sheer hard work and determination.

The real reward came years later when I overheard my daughter telling a friend she was going to college to earn two degrees, just like her mother.

Remember, if your "why" isn't strong enough yet, **"REST IF YOU MUST, BUT DON'T YOU QUIT."**

About Adrienna Harris

 Adrienna Harris graduated from Winston-Salem State University with a dual undergraduate degree in Management Information System and Accounting. After graduating from college, she has held different IT related jobs throughout the system development life cycle. She has also earned her MBA, with a focus on Leadership and Strategy, from Wake Forest University. Throughout her career, she has demonstrated a profound commitment to leveraging data-driven insights to enhance business operations and drive strategic decision-making.

Adrienna was recognized for her contributions to the community through her involvement in the Civic Leadership Academy. This initiative has allowed her to work with other leaders and foster a culture of civic engagement, further underscoring her dedication to leadership and community service.

Adrienna founded a company called I Need to Know How, LLC. This company focuses on providing how-to content and videos for around the house, crafts, DIY, and more. To give back to the community, it will provide videos for students to learn about different math subjects like basic math, algebra, and geometry. (ineedtoknowhow.com)

To get Adrienna's gift: www.LOTbook.net/gift/Adrienna

For the Love of Transformation

Loving Yourself is Your Superpower

By Ken Patterson

Loving yourself is the single most important thing that you can do to unlock your "Superpower" so you can live a life that most people only dream of. It is one of the greatest things you can do for yourself, those you love, and the world around you.

Loving yourself affects everything you do and everyone you meet. It affects your relationships, your finances, how you see the world, and how the world sees you. Everything is affected by whether you love yourself.

Why is loving yourself your Superpower? Because it can open a whole new world to you, filled with magic and beauty and help you love what you already have more than you ever thought possible. It can even open doors you thought were closed. Activating your Superpower will help you see your potential in a whole new light. When you love yourself, you:

- Consider how you feel first, before anyone else.
- Value your time and it becomes more precious to you.
- Hang out with people that lift you up, not tear you down.
- Have understanding and compassion for yourself.
- Talk nicely to yourself.
- Make choices based on what is important to you.
- Take chances you would not take because of outside influences.

In this chapter, I will share a few of the many processes I have used and taught to people just like you on how to love themselves and unlock their Superpower. Now it's your turn!

To love yourself, appreciating or feeling better about anything is a great place to begin. Here's how it works; the better you feel, the better you can feel. It builds on itself. Appreciation is one of the most powerful energies on the planet. It is a mathematical principle and a powerful way to love yourself. What you appreciate appreciates and then that appreciates on top of that, it builds and multiplies.

What really makes it so powerful is that it takes so little of it, like plutonium, it's so potent. When you appreciate anything, and I mean anything, it will multiply. Here are examples of things that you can easily appreciate, to help you get started:

- A dog playing in the park.
- The wind blowing through the trees.
- A baby making cute faces.
- Being able to drive your car.
- The breath in your lungs.
- Being able to read.
- There is something about yourself that you can appreciate, like your hair, your eyes, or how you handle things.
- A natural gift like playing the guitar.
- A spiritual gift.

Appreciating anything can really change how you feel. You are not trying to appreciate something that you don't appreciate right now. You can't force yourself to feel something you don't, even as much as people try. Like my grandpappy used to say, "A person convinced against his will is of the same opinion still."

As you look for more things to appreciate, then you can set the stage for more opportunities to look at yourself in a better light because you are flowing in a higher vibration, at a higher vantage point. You are looking for love in all the right places.

When you are looking for things to appreciate, you are looking for simple things to feel good about so you can shift your energy and vibration. You can get to the bigger stuff another time, because if you try to appreciate something that you have mixed feelings about like money, your career, or your health, it could open a bag of tricks-or-treats or Pandora's box.

Remember, simplicity often leads to the best results. Here is one way you can add a bit of jet fuel to this process to magnify your results until you get more used to doing it. Whenever anything good happens to you that you can add your official stamp of "appreciation" to, milk the heck out of it. Like a freaking cow. Here's how:

- Talk about it.
- Write about it.
- Tell a friend about it.

- Think about it.
- Go over it in your mind.
- Hold on to it for as long as you can, like the way a comedian will keep bringing up a joke told early in the performance to get laughs again and again.

Here are some easily overlooked examples of when you can milk it. When someone does something nice unexpectedly, when you get a gift, when somebody lets you go first in a checkout line, washes your window at the gas station, or gives you a discount on a purchase without a coupon... milk it.

The longer you take the time to appreciate things, the more you'll notice new things showing up in your life to be thankful for. Remember, appreciation multiplies. Incredible things will happen, and from my experience, I can tell you—it flat out works.

Your Emotional GPS

Another way to unlock your Superpower, and this one is built into you already, and I call it your "EPS" Emotional Positioning System. And very much like the "GPS" on your phone or in your car, it can tell you where you are relative to where you want to be. You may ask, why is this important?

If you want to go somewhere, you first need to know where you are. Want to feel better, then knowing where you are emotionally is just as important as knowing where you are physically to take a trip. If you called a travel agent and said I want to go somewhere, one of the first things they would ask is, where are you coming from and where do you want to go?

So just like using your GPS when wanting to travel somewhere,

you can activate your EPS and ask yourself "how do I really feel" and don't sugar coat it. Be honest with yourself. Really tune into "you" for a moment to get a powerful signal, just like having four bars on your phone or tuning into a radio station.

You may know exactly what emotion you feel, for example anxiety, hopelessness, optimism, frustration, unworthiness.... You may just feel off or you just don't feel good or right, or you just don't feel like yourself, or uncomfortable or bad. These are general and that's perfectly ok. You'll get better at understanding your emotions with a little practice.

Knowing where you are now in relationship to where you want to be helps you to cruise up the emotional scale and feel better. Before I share how you can get to a better feeling place, let's get a better understanding of your emotions on a scale that can help guide you to figure out where you are and where you want to be.

What's the emotional scale? In short, emotions that feel bad, like fear, unworthiness, grief, despair, and powerlessness, are on the bottom part of the scale and have the lowest vibration.

Emotions that feel good, like joy, appreciation, freedom, love, and empowerment, are on the top part of the scale and have the highest vibration. And, of course, there is every other emotion and vibration in between. Once you are aware of where you are, then you can do something about it.

Here are examples of what you can do to feel better:

- Take a walk, take a nap, or call an encouraging friend.
- Change your clothes, take a drive, or take a shower.
- Watch a hilarious movie or listen to your favorite music.

Anything that can interrupt the broadcast of negative thoughts and feelings so that you can feel better. With a little practice, you will develop a proclivity, or a strength in this area, which makes it easier to get back to who you really are, which I believe is love, and where all your Superpower is.

You May Be Wondering

At this point…You may be wondering, have I ever "not" loved myself or had a real serious problem with loving me and being who I really am? The answer is, absolutely yes.

In fact, as I was growing up and for many years as an adult, I thought there was a malfunction in me, like God just had a bad day on the day I was created, and really messed up. I felt like I just didn't fit in, like I was a freak or something that had no business being here.

Then there were some questions that really moved the needle for me like, "Isn't life supposed to be way better than this?"

So, I started asking myself more questions. The better the questions, the better the answers. I realized that many of my beliefs and paradigms—while not all bad—had negative aspects that were just a load of garbage. I finally understood that there was never anything wrong with me, and there never had been, period.

And the truth is there is nothing wrong with you,

never was, never will be.

You are an infinite being, you are life in a bottle, you are the cosmos walking around with shorts, a t-shirt, and flip-flops, or in a dress with high heels, or whatever. The point is, you are a phenomenal creation of the highest form, an extension, and expression of God, Creation, Source, Guardian Angels, Higher Power or whatever you call it. That divine creation is you!

What Helped Me?

In reflecting on what helped me the most, during the difficult times in my life, I found that evaluating what served me and what didn't serve me really helped me understand my Superpower. Questions that you can ask yourself are:

- Am I at the top of my list?
- What builds me up?

- What encourages me?
- What challenges me?
- What do I love doing?
- What feeds me?
- What am I getting from outside myself?
- What am I getting from family, friends, Facebook, and Tick Tock?

Whatever you are paying attention to, clicking on, and spending time with is also spending time with you. What you are into is into you as well. It is related to what you get back. That's why they call it your "feed." It's food for thought.

In so many ways we are taught, spoon fed really, by well-meaning friends, family, social media, and peers that we need to go outside of ourselves to be loved and understood. I am not knocking any of these, but you may have emotional heartburn or a gag reflex from them without even realizing it. It's amazing what can go on behind the scenes.

Therefore, asking questions regularly about what does and doesn't serve you and how it is affecting you is so valuable. Only you can truly know.

Self-Love Reflection Technique

The last technique I want to share has helped me and many others learn to love themselves more, and you don't even have to believe it will work. I call it the Self-Love Reflection Technique, or SLR, and yes, it involves using a mirror.

It's safe to say you've probably looked in the mirror to check if your hair is in place or if those dark circles are more noticeable today. You might wonder what others will think about your outfit—whether that dress, shirt, or pair of boots is the right choice. And yes, you've likely asked yourself, "Does this make me look fat?"

Some reasons you can't or don't want to look in a mirror for any length of time are because you feel unworthy or not good enough. There is such power in being able to look at yourself with loving eyes, without all the judgments and criticisms that you may have when looking at your reflection.

The SLR technique can be remarkably effective in helping you love yourself, and it works even if you don't believe it. You can do it with any mirror, including a compact or cellphone mirror. It only takes a few seconds, and it gets easier with practice. It really is not complicated at all.

Some of the many benefits that you can expect from doing SLR are feeling more self-confident, less depressed, less anxious, and more comfortable in your own skin. SLR can easily be done anywhere at any time. I recommend doing it two times a day if possible. The bathroom is a great place because you go in there a couple times a day.

Find a mirror in a quiet place where you can be alone. Look into the mirror, preferably into your eyes, as best you can, and this can sometimes be hard. It's ok, you will get the hang of it. Now speak aloud this affirmation to yourself.

"I totally and entirely love, forgive, and accept you,

right here, right now. "

There are many affirmations that you can use. The one I have used for years is "I totally and entirely love, forgive and accept you, right here, right now" while looking at myself in the eyes and pointing at myself. It helps to pick one eye instead of going back and forth between eyes. You can alter it or change it completely, use whatever resonates most with you.

Experts recommend practicing it for 28 to 45 days to form a habit and replace negative self-talk with positive affirmations. You are rewriting a program. Therefore, you don't have to believe it will work, because you are using the power of making a habit to override possible disbeliefs or judgments.

Now that you have these simple processes, I hope they help you and that you enjoy the journey to loving yourself and unlocking your Superpower. If this chapter resonates with you, you are going to love my gift.

About Ken Patterson

 Ken Patterson is a certified Transformational Life Coach with over 35 years of experience dedicated to empowering individuals to embrace their authentic self, overcome obstacles, and realize their full potential.

As the founder of Youtopia LLC, he specializes in providing practical strategies that enable individuals to cultivate self-love and transform their lives through a diverse range of study, experience, and disciplines, including the Law of Attraction, Quantum Physics, EFT, Brain Science, Near-Death Experiences, Self-Development, Human Behavior, Spirituality, Religion, and Theology. This extensive background equips him with a unique perspective and a holistic approach to personal transformation.

Ken has touched the lives of many, guiding them toward self-discovery and a more fulfilling existence. His commitment to nurturing personal growth and well-being makes him a valuable resource for anyone seeking to enhance their life experience. Through one-on-one coaching, public speaking, and workshops, Ken continues to inspire and motivate individuals on their journey back to themselves, where true happiness is.

To get Ken's gift, go to: www.LOTbook.net/gift/Ken

Made in the USA
Monee, IL
10 June 2026

53029992R00136